SIR EDWIN LUTYENS

SIR EDWIN LUTYENS

Britain's Greatest Architect?

CLIVE ASLET

TRIGLYPH
BOOKS

First published in the United Kingdom in 2024 by Triglyph Books.

Triglyph Books
154 Tachbrook Street
London SW1V 2NE
www.triglyphbooks.com

Instagram: @triglyphbooks

Publisher: Clive Aslet and Dylan Thomas
Production Manager: Kate Turner
Design and typesetting: Tetragon, London
Cover design: Ocky Murray
Research Assistant: Rebecca Lilley
Copyeditor: Henry Howard
Proofreader: Mike Turner

British Library Cataloguing-in-Publication Data.

A catalogue record for this book is available from the British Library.

ISBN : 978–1–7397314–3-4

Printed and bound sustainably in China.

To the members of
The Lutyens Trust
and
The Lutyens Trust America

'There is that in art which transcends all rules, it is the divine.'

LUTYENS WRITING TO HIS
WIFE LADY EMILY IN 1907

'Lutyens possessed the faculty of making everybody feel much younger.'

HAROLD NICOLSON IN
THE SPECTATOR, JANUARY 7, 1944

Contents

Introduction

L UTYENS HAS BEEN CALLED THE GREATEST ARCHITECT that Britain has ever produced. Of course there are other candidates, but let me argue the claim; it rests on four pillars. First comes his three-dimensional imagination which enabled him to conjure thrilling spaces and volumes out of almost any commission. Only Lutyens would have insisted on the minute diminution made by successive courses of rustication as they go up the façade of the Midland Bank in Poultry, despite the trouble it caused his draughtsmen. Other rusticated façades around the world are strictly vertical – not this one.

Secondly, turning to the two-and-a-half-thousand-year-old tradition of Classicism, the system of proportion and ornament that originated in Ancient Greece and Rome, he did not simply borrow a language from previous architects but reinvented it. This was partly to adapt the old means of expression to the new building types of the twentieth century, such as war memorials and large office buildings. It was also because he had to in order to satisfy his love of elemental, austere forms and his reverence for geometry. For Lutyens, the perfection of the sphere seems to have held a spiritual meaning; it provided a glimpse of the divine.

Thirdly, Lutyens found an architectural means of expressing some of the big ideas of his time.

In the 1890s and 1900s, his country houses created a domestic self-image for the Edwardian age, an idyll at a time of social change and technological innovation. The palace that he built for the imperial viceroy at New Delhi – well-ordered, calm, its footprint bigger than Versailles – is a built representation of the lofty idealism about Empire that motivated his countrymen – or some of them, in their better moments. Before New Delhi was completed in 1931, he had created many of Britain's most important war memorials and war cemeteries, notably the Cenotaph on Whitehall and the Thiepval Arch on the Somme. They were abstract, geometrical, devoid of religious imagery – and yet they were immediately seen as an appropriate focus for the national agony of grief.

Fourthly, as can be seen from Carl Laubin's caprice of Lutyens's principal works – *Metiendo Vivendum* – used as the endpapers of this book, he built a huge amount in a long career, estimated at around five hundred and fifty significant commissions. And the range, as well as the size, was immense. Town houses, institutional buildings, churches, offices, a cathedral of epic proportions (admittedly only the crypt was built), the fountains in Trafalgar Square, a host of ingenious small structures – a village shelter at Mells to remember a dead child, a belvedere for Gertrude Jekyll to watch thunderstorms sweep over the South Downs, a reservoir head on Dartmoor known as the Pimple. No other architect has been so various.

For all that, this is a short biography. It does not aim to be comprehensive; instead I have concentrated on a small number of works which illustrate different aspects of his achievement. Some readers might wish for a longer one, and two have already been provided. The first was Christopher Hussey's incomparable *Life of Sir Edwin Lutyens* published in 1950, six years after the architect's death: surely the greatest architectural biography ever written. Nearly half a century later, Jane Ridley brought out *The Architect and his Wife: A Life of Edwin Lutyens*, a worthy successor (which is saying something), written *con brio* and *con amore* by the architect's great-granddaughter: psychology, motivation, sex, clients, money – subjects that were off limits to Hussey could be discussed with a new frankness in 2002. Both are five or six hundred-pagers, both out of print. Who knows? In time a brave author may attempt to add a third full-scale biography, but that day has not dawned yet; whoever undertakes it will have to face decades of research without a certain prospect of adding much to the general story. It would daunt many a writer. And one must not forget that biographies on the heroic scale, now expected of the genre, ask a lot of the reader. I would like this volume to introduce Lutyens to as many people as possible, and that is another reason for keeping it short.

Lutyens opened his first office in 1889 at the age of nineteen – a precocious age, given that many architects do not find their feet before they are forty. Putting his bicycle in the guard's van of the train from London, he would pedal to sites around Surrey, full of energy, lyricism and jokes. His many country houses, often in the Home Counties, were a rhapsody to the English landscape amid which he had grown up. Under the tutelage of the craftswoman and gardener Gertrude Jekyll, he thrilled to the old, hand-made culture of the country people whose way of life was fast disappearing, while at the same time finding fun in its quaintness. Card-carrying members of the Arts and Crafts Movement strove to be ostentatiously dull: Lutyens was irrepressible, a master of form and a poet of materials. This was expensive architecture for rich people, which gave him an unhelpful reputation for extravagance. As his thirties wore on, he sought a bigger canvas. Hampstead Garden Suburb gave him two churches to design, and from there, with little other public architecture or planning experience under his belt, he made the leap to the Viceroy's House and New Delhi. They came in 1912. It was, however, the First World War which enabled – indeed, forced on him – a shift in gear. The country-house practice dried up. In its place arose an aching need for monuments that would pay respect to the Fallen. Thousands were erected across Britain, the Empire and the battlefields of France and Flanders. Unusually, Lutyens believed that the most appropriate form they could take would be abstract, a matter of geometrical proportion and little else: an architecture stripped of most ornament and devoid of overt symbolism. This was surely remarkable in an age habituated to great military parades and the pomp of Edwardian Baroque; but it was immediately understood by the millions of people in the country who had lost sons, husbands and brothers. It was for his unpaid work for the Imperial War Graves Commission, as well as the design of New Delhi, that he was knighted in 1918.

In the early works, we can glimpse Lutyens's love of the abstract in his insistence on an exact angle for roofs – 54 degrees and 45 minutes: the beauty of this pitch was that it created a hip or corner of 45 degrees, which made the job of carpenters easier on site. Despite a lack of formal education in mathematics, he was fascinated – to an almost occult extent – by numbers. Ratios and proportions are the stuff of Classicism, the High Game which enthralled him after 1905. But in a plastic form, we can feel the aesthetic excitement of geometry even more thrillingly in – of all things – the castle on Dartmoor which Lutyens reluctantly built for Julius Drewe: Castle Drogo is better understood as a gigantic piece of sculpture than as a country house, let alone a family home. After the First World War, Lutyens's greatest works transcend the conventions of Classicism to become works of mathematics – pure form of the most inventive and cerebral kind.[1] His masterpiece of the 1930s, the unbuilt Roman Catholic Cathedral at Liverpool, revisits previous themes, such as the triumphal arch motif which he used in a bravely original way at Thiepval, which were then developed with the complexity of a Bach fugue; although never completed, his titanic vision continues to amaze visitors to the seventeen-foot-long model that exists in the Museum of Liverpool. Not a conventionally religious man, Lutyens was, at the end of his life, happy in the company of the Jesuits for whom he designed the monastic Campion Hall in Oxford. He said it was his best building. Aspects of Campion Hall reprise the Surrey style with which Lutyens started his long career. In 1942, he became the first architect to be awarded the Order of Merit. Two years later he died.

These achievements were only possible because people needed and could pay for his buildings. 'There will never be great architects without great patrons,' Lutyens wrote in 1915.[2] His clients provide a window through which to view the age in which he lived. With that in mind I have attempted to give a broad picture of both his career and the times. But rather than attempting to describe every building on a crowded stage, I have directed a spotlight onto a small number of the projects that seem to me interesting or characteristic, leaving the others to dart in and out of the shadows as supporting members of the cast.

I was introduced to Lutyens when I joined *Country Life* as an architectural writer in 1977. Not long before, the magazine had moved from the offices that Lutyens designed for it in Tavistock Street, Covent Garden, to an ugly high-rise office block in Southwark, officially called King's Reach Tower but popularly known as Fawlty Towers. The staff seemed like one of the lost tribes of Israel, bitter in the lamentations over the glory from which they were now exiled. This was in some respects strange, since the working conditions in the old building had become cramped, as the demands of the company expanded. While the editor had a grand office, smaller fry were crammed into cubbyholes. (Perhaps it had always been rather like that. Lutyens did not trouble himself too much about servants' quarters.) Within memory, heavy printing presses had clanked in the basement while the compositors set type in the airy lightness of the attic – whence the cry would come down to the sub-editors for another half inch of poetry to fill out the allotted space. For the sort of folk who worked on *Country Life*, the Tavistock Street office was a paradise. There were keystones representing the seasons over the windows, flamboyant CL monograms on the glass and brass chandeliers in the hall; a lot of the furniture had been specially designed by Lutyens, including, it was thought, a set of spider-back chairs whose prickly horsehair upholstery, authentically renewed by my predecessor as editor, was unpopular with female colleagues in skirts.[3] The green-painted, Chinese Chippendale vitrines in the editor's office were so tall that they could not fit into the dismal, low-ceilinged rooms of King's Reach Tower; after some years in storage they were sold.

The *Country Life* building was but the outward expression of the magazine's self-identification with Lutyens. As I describe in chapter 3, Edward Hudson, the magazine's founder, had been convinced of Lutyens's genius: *Country Life* published nearly every major work that he produced. *Country Life* and Lutyens suited each other. The one was a deeply British magazine, the other a no less British architect – if British, for this purpose, incorporates the British Empire. For years the *Country Life* picture library, with its large glass negatives, owned the only photographs of Lutyens's work that were readily available for publication: I was among many visitors surprised to discover that houses like Tigbourne Court were in reality much smaller than the heroic black-and-white images of the magazine's Edwardian photographer Charles Latham. Some of the wackier buildings were left out of the *Country Life* canon, but not many. There must have been numerous behind-the-scenes conversations as well. For a while, Hudson and Lutyens had London houses next to each other in Queen Anne's Gate. Lutyens was in *Country Life*'s DNA. His era had been a glorious one for the magazine: it had been a period of excitement in the world that it covered, which gave it purpose. There was nothing *Country Life* could contribute to the Swinging Sixties, or the chaotic Seventies for that matter. Colleagues in the architectural department kept their faith with Lutyens but it was that of a minority cult, like the magazine's devotion to niceties of form that had little currency elsewhere (the subheads of the country-house articles made careful distinctions between THE HOME OF MR AND MRS X; THE SEAT OF LORD AND LADY Y; or A SEAT OF THE DUKE AND DUCHESS OF Z – note the indefinite article).

Before the exhibition simply called 'Lutyens' opened at the Hayward Gallery in 1981, cult members revered him as part of a lost civilisation, the return of which seemed doubtful at best; he was the symbol of an aesthetic conservatism that was the antithesis of Modernist ideology. That did him a disservice. In the 1930s he thought it was 'inevitable and right' that architecture should be influenced by steel construction, reinforced concrete and 'mechanical contrivances' – here was 'youthful glamour striving after something fresh, something better,' just as he and his contemporaries had 'tried to produce fresher and better things.' He deeply regretted the passing of 'humanism and the personal note' in the work of traditional bricklayers, masons and joiners as makers of buildings, but did not make such a fool of himself over it as did the architect Reginald Blomfield or the painter Alfred Munnings.[4] Neither his early years nor, for that matter, those of *Country Life* had been wholly conservative. The magazine was never a political organ but, still, it is worth saying that it was founded by Liberals and central to the Liberal Party was land reform, which put it at odds with the generally Conservative owners of the landed estates surrounding traditional country houses. Lutyens would have built for anyone (and did so for the crooked financier Whitaker Wright who swallowed cyanide at the Old Bailey shortly after being convicted for fraud) but his clients were rarely Conservative diehards, except in Spain.[5] As for his own political views, never strong, he seems to have begun Liberal and veered towards a romantic Toryism of the kind espoused by his friend Detmar Blow, who ate, in an egalitarian way, with the servants, much as Lutyens insisted that whoever visited his office in Delhi should eat at his table whatever their colour; but that was very different from the Conservatives at Westminster – he would have rather voted Labour than for them.[6]

The Arcadia of his country houses was romantic, nostalgic but new. They were new kinds of houses, with a few dozen acres of garden rather than full-blown estates, glossy automobiles in the 'motor stable', and all the innovations of the turn-of-the-twentieth century domestic technology; most of them were really villas, extravagantly rural in appearance but supported by money that did not come from the land. Even nostalgia – the regret for the passing of the old home-made, horse-powered, smock-wearing countryside of rush-bottomed chairs and straw beehives – was new. So was collecting brown furniture and other antiques with an eye to authenticity and patina. War memorials and war cemeteries, when the need for them arose after the Great War, were also new: there had been nothing like the Cenotaph, the Thiepval Arch, war cemeteries such as Étaples or Monchy in the Pas-de-Calais, or even village war memorials, before 1914. They were a new building type which Lutyens approached in a wholly original way. New too were the planning of New Delhi and the architecture of the Viceroy's House, however much it has since come to seem the last hurrah of a doomed institution.

New for the Edwardian age was the attitude to the past expressed in the country house. As Timothy Brittain-Catlin observes, for the first time in British history people built houses that were purposefully made to look old, often incorporating the core of a genuine old building – and adopting its style – as they did so.[7] Lutyens took to this way of doing things with gusto. It lent itself to historical teases. While his 1906 contribution to Folly Farm in Berkshire was in a seventeenth-century manner, when he revisited six years later, he reverted to Surrey vernacular, thus appearing to move chronologically backwards rather than forwards. Lutyens played with history throughout his career, and not only in country houses. Mezzanine windows in the façade of the Theosophical Society on Tavistock Square peep over the ashlar of the ground floor, as though they were an afterthought – an impression reinforced by the blind reveals of what read as earlier windows above them. Occasionally and somewhat reluctantly he would introduce genuine pieces of old architecture from somewhere else, as in the timber-framed houses that were incorporated into Great Dixter and the Manor House at Ashby St Ledgers. More often he mixed styles within the same building, drawing on different periods and sources at the same time. Lutyens did not invent this kind of eclecticism. It was everywhere at the turn of the twentieth century, in what architectural historians have dubbed the Freestyle. As the architect Arthur Edmund Street put it in 1901, 'The designer skips from century to century, or stands with his feet wide apart while the ages roll between.'[8] But Lutyens outperformed his contemporaries in terms of daring and zest. Take Little Thakeham, where the architecture of what one might think of as a medieval great hall has not only been reinterpreted in Baroque idiom but represented in stone, as though the outside of the house has barged into the domestic spaces – the bravura is breathtaking. Initially, Lutyens had no truck with Indian architecture when designing New Delhi: he believed that the verities of Classicism were universal and eternal. Circumstances forced him to modify his design, the result being an amalgam of East and West. This is part of its brilliance. He may have resented the need to do it but the ability to speak several stylistic languages at once was something he had mastered early on.

Lutyens's borrowings might be compared to Mozart's habit of picking up themes from other composers – Handel in parts of the Requiem, for instance – and running with them in his own way.

Much as Lutyens worshipped Sir Christopher Wren, he never copied him, even in the building that became the British School at Rome, which he was required by the terms of his commission to model on the upper storey of the west front of St Paul's. Next door to the Wren church of St James's, Piccadilly, Lutyens's jewel-like Midland Bank was inspired by Sanmicheli. His Classicism is inventive – witness the planning of country houses, which never provide an axial view from front door to garden, despite their symmetrical façades. As it happens, Lutyens was late to the Wren party. By 1905, when his work took a decisively Classical direction, the only original thing about his 'Wrennaissance' was the pun; architects such as John Brydon and Herbert Baker had been advocating Wren as the foundation of a national style for the previous fifteen years.[9] But Lutyens was brilliant where many of his contemporaries, similarly committed to the Arts and Crafts ideal of sound building, were stodgy. On the face of it, the Oxford mathematician and astronomer Wren and the largely unschooled Lutyens could hardly have been less like each other. But Lutyens taught himself enough about geometry to make elaborate calculations for the entasis of the Cenotaph and the war stone of the Imperial War Graves cemeteries on the Western Front. And there was one way in which the two men were alike: both were lucky. They lived at a time of great opportunities for architecture – in Wren's case, following the Great Fire of London, in Lutyens's, with the building of a new imperial capital in India and the need to memorialise the Great War.

In life, Lutyens hid his personality behind a fusillade of witticisms and puns, which could become tiresome as he grew older; he hated speaking in public and rarely appeared in print. His daughter Mary Lutyens was the first to lift the veil. Writing so soon after his death, Hussey was understandably blind to his subject's egotism. Of course, great artists cannot function without self-belief – arrogance if you like – and considerable amounts of 'me-time'. But

Lutyens's ruthlessness can be disturbing. He captivated potential clients and mercilessly beguiled them into spending more than they had intended on building his tours de force. When Lutyens was about to be appointed as architect of the British Embassy in Washington, a senior Treasury official warned of his reputation as 'an extremely extravagant architect who doesn't care what he lets his client in for'. It was a fair point. Estimates were routinely exceeded. When John Stewart's *Herbert Baker: Architect to the British Empire* appeared in 2021, the brutality with which Lutyens treated his old friend and collaborator in pursuit of his architectural vision was laid bare. Artistically he was right, but it does not make for attractive reading. He was famously unscrupulous in poaching jobs from other architects; he was probably right to think that he could do them better but it was professionally unethical, nonetheless. Even today, some families in Liverpool remember the Roman Catholic Cathedral not as the greatest church that was never built but as a drain on poor households, as parish priests extracted penny contributions to construct a dome that would have been bigger than St Peter's.

Despite Lutyens's extravagance with his clients' money, he was close with his own. His staff were meanly paid. And the Lutyens who could captivate the children of his clients with his whimsy had little time for his own; he saw them only on Sundays. They were left to the care of his undomestic wife Lady Emily who was equally selfish in her pursuit of Theosophy and the beautiful Indian boy Krishnamurti, its Chosen One. Mary Lutyens got her own back on her parents by opening the bedroom door and describing their relationship: he adoring, puppyish and sexually inconsiderate, she deserted by his constant round of country-house visits, blind to architecture and unsatisfied in bed. Strangely, the children seem always to have loved their batty, irresponsible mother, while regarding their endlessly punning father as an embarrassment and a buffoon. 'I cannot love him,' wrote the seventeen-year-old Mary as her mother whisked her from India to join some dubious Theosophical cultists in Australia. 'He works and slaves from dawn till dark.'[10]

I have said that Lutyens did more than anyone to shape the Edwardians' domestic self-image – I should, however, qualify that comment. Not all members of the plutocracy had romantic instincts. Every bodily comfort could be met by decorating firms such as Lenygon and Morant or Charles Mellier & Co.: the opulence of their deep-sprung upholstery has never been exceeded. Luxury of this kind was alien to the Arts and Crafts Movement but even so, some progressive architects (notably M.H. Baillie Scott) created beautiful interiors that were delicious to live in. This was never Lutyens's way. After the privations of his eccentric, solitary childhood, his domestic ideal was austere – not as doctrinally hair-shirt as the puritan C.F.A. Voysey's, but hard surfaces predominate. The decorators whom he most liked to work with were the brothers Frederick and George Muntzer, and they were firmly in the Voysey camp, with their patently hand-hewn chairs and scrubbed oak table tops, best seen at Lambay, one of Lutyens's favourite jobs. After a week's stay at Lindisfarne Castle, Lytton Strachey judged it 'very dark, with nowhere to sit, and nothing but stone under, over and round you, which produced a distressing effect … No, not a comfortable place by any means.' The spectacular hall at Little Thakeham – the main living space of the house – must have been impossible to keep warm. Lady Lytton's room at a corner of Homewood with two outside walls was so cold it was known as Vladivostok. Lutyens chimneys often smoked. The colour-palette was not that of Nature, the default of the Arts and Crafts Movement: shiny black ceilings, red lacquered walls and emerald green floors provided a foretaste of Art Deco which must have been unnerving to weaker spirits at the time.

Although Lutyens was a fashionable architect, who would cajole and flatter clients into building projects they did not always wholly want and sometimes regretted, he never pandered to the baser instincts of humanity by making his homes easy to live in. This became particularly obvious after the First World War: few concessions were made to the shortage of servants – or at New Delhi for the imminent end of the Empire for which he was creating, at great expense, so majestic a capital.

The man himself never entirely outgrew the pinched circumstances of his childhood, when his clothes were handed down from his brothers and his hair resembled a haystack. Long after most of that hair had disappeared, he would still trim the remnant himself, twisting a strand of it into a tight little rope and snipping it off with nail scissors. Although less successful architects regarded him jealously as having made a lot of money, 'his natural generosity and the extravagant tastes of his family combined to relieve him of most of his earnings,' remembered Daphne Pollen, daughter of his client-friends Cecil and Maude Baring; '… he spent nothing on himself; his suits were shiny and his hands grimy.'[11] Almost his only relaxation, other than drawing funny doodles, was the solitary card game patience. It is possible that he would now be considered to have had obsessive or even mildly autistic tendencies, traits that are often associated with genius.

Writing in 1950, Hussey felt that 'the Thiepval Memorial, the Poultry bank, and the designs for Liverpool Cathedral constitute forward bases, of great cogency, established by Lutyens's genius as starting points for the advance of the Humanist tradition into the questionable future.' In other words, a School of Lutyens could develop to provide the second half of the twentieth century with monuments and large commercial buildings within the Western tradition of architecture. If only. Lutyens's sun went into all but total eclipse after his death in 1944. To doctrinaire Modernists, his lyricism, wit, love of handwork and beautiful materials, association with Empire, and relative detachment from the social objects of the day made him a horror (his one and only design for workers' housing, the Page Street Flats with their cheerful chequerboard walls, flagrantly committed the Modernist sin of façadism). They might not have minded if, like many Arts and Crafts architects, he had struggled to find clients, but his commercial success and popularity turned even the memory of him into a threat. That changed when the Modernist hegemony was brought down by the rise of Postmodernism. Tentatively, ornament returned to favour – but only if it was used with irony, as though in quotation marks. Although Lutyens was awarded the Gold Medal of the Institute of American Architects in 1925, he built only one work in the United States – the British Embassy in Washington, whose difficult, sloping site brought forth one of his most brilliant plans. Nevertheless, it was American architects, such as the Postmodernists Robert Venturi and Denise Scott Brown and the Classicist Allan Greenberg who first championed him, publishing articles from the 1960s. In Britain, the gallery-going public was enthralled by the 'Lutyens' exhibition of 1981–2, which transformed the bunker-like interior of the Hayward Gallery into a succession of Lutyens-inspired spaces designed by Piers Gough. Numerous books appeared, some of the most notable being Mary Lutyens's biography in 1980, Robert Grant Irving's *Indian Summer: Lutyens, Baker and Imperial Delhi*, 1981, Clayre Percy and Jane Ridley's *The Letters of Edwin Lutyens to his Wife, Lady Emily*, 1985, Jane Brown's *Lutyens and the Edwardians, An English Architect and his Clients*, 1996, and Jane Ridley's *The Architect and his Wife: a Life of Edwin Lutyens*, 2002. There have also been major works on most of Lutyens's contemporaries. However, as Chair of the Lutyens Trust (founded to secure Lutyens's memory after the Hayward Gallery exhibition) I cannot help noticing, not only that the rate of publication has slowed (which may not necessarily be a bad thing) but that his name does not have the general currency that it did at the end of the twentieth century. Lutyens saw himself as belonging to a 'humanist generation' in which 'the measure of man's architecture was man'; his work for the Imperial War Graves Commission shows that he respected people of every creed. But in common with most of his contemporaries, he was not obviously 'woke'; to a certain kind of historian, his wife Emily, whose socialism and immersion in Theosophy were a source of distress to Lutyens and not helpful to his career, may now be the more interesting figure. I find that architect friends in America are more convinced of his genius than the generality of their peers in the UK. Over here, young architects, architectural historians and the general public are missing out.

Le Bois des Moutiers, at Varengeville, on the Normandy coast, not published by *Country Life* until Clive Aslet wrote about it in 1982. The Mallets were introduced to Lutyens by his wife Lady Emily's aunt, and it was at Le Bois des Moutiers that Lady Emily was introduced to Theosophy.

Since 1981, when I produced *Country Life*'s first brace of articles on Le Bois des Moutiers, I have been writing and thinking about Lutyens on a fairly continuous basis. This book gathers together the thoughts and observations that have come to me during that time. I dwell longest on aspects that offer new material due to the archives I have recently consulted, notably at Castle Drogo, Mells Manor, the Churchill Archives Centre at Cambridge, the HSBC Archives, which hold the archives of the Midland Bank, and Campion Hall. I am grateful to all the country-house owners, curators and librarians who have made me welcome. For obvious reasons I know rather a lot about *Country Life* and its founder Edward Hudson. More has come to light about Herbert Johnson, owner of Marsh Court and one of Lutyens's favourite clients, than was available to previous biographers.

I have gained enormously by visiting his buildings in company with architects like Tom Kligerman, Oliver Cope, Michael Imber and Michael Graham, as well as *Country Life*'s incomparable architectural editor John Goodall. I am grateful to John and *Country Life*'s editor Mark Hedges for continuing to commission articles on Lutyens, each of which demands fresh research. Lockdown inspired an excellent series of webinars by the Lutyens Trust America, which (still available online and highly recommended) are full of fresh insights. Dr Robin Prater, executive director of the LTA, has organised many wonderful Lutyens tours which I have been lucky enough to join, most recently to Lambay. On this side of the Atlantic, fellow Trustees of the Lutyens Trust, including Martin Lutyens, Jane Ridley, Charles Hind, Mervyn Miller and Paul Waite, have widened my horizons in many ways. Paul's tours for the LT are unforgettable, not least the week in Spain that he masterminded with his husband Francisco Javier Orjales-Mourente in the spring of 2023. This book has been an opportunity for me to assemble the lessons I have learnt from these and other disparate sources.

Without caring owners there would be no Lutyens buildings to study, and I am hugely grateful to those who have allowed me to visit their properties over the years. They include the Clark family at Munstead Wood; Lord and Lady Cobbold at Knebworth; the National Trust at Lindisfarne Castle and Castle Drogo; the owner's team at Marsh Court; Lord Revelstoke, Millie Baring and Louis Jebb at Lambay; the Hon. Michael and Mrs Samuel at Park House, Mells; Lord and Lady Oxford and Asquith at Mells Manor; David Davidson at the Hampstead Garden Suburb Trust; and Revd Dr Nick Austin SJ, Master of Campion Hall Oxford. There have been many others since my interest took wing and I would like to thank all of them, if not always by name, for their time and hospitality.

I have been fortunate in having a publisher to hand in Triglyph Books, the publishing house which Dylan Thomas and I founded in 2019. Dylan has been undeniable in his desire for me to get the book written and I am grateful to him for offering the facilities of our press. During the process I have been buoyed up by the enthusiasm of my Triglyph colleagues, including Kate Turner, India Brooker, Ines Cross and Leona Crawford, and have been lucky to have had the help of my son Johnny to share some of the load. Rebecca Lilley is the paragon of research assistants; as a former secretary of the Lutyens Trust, she came to the project with an unrivalled prior knowledge of the subject and has been invaluable in pursuing new sources of research. Cathryn Spence, the current secretary of the Lutyens Trust, has provided constant help and support. Other friends and historians whose have generously shared knowledge and insights are David Avrill, Hugh Petter, Candia Lutyens, Martin Lutyens, Charles Hind, Alan Powers, Mary Miers, Bea Reeve-Tucker and Gareth Banner at The Ned, Hugh Byrne,

Peter Davidson, Diarmaid MacCulloch, David Pearson, Steven Pollock Hill, Ben Dale, Erica Williamson, Annabel Watts and Bryher Mason.

John Goodall, Tim Brittain-Catlin and Rebecca Lilley have read the manuscript, making many important observations and steering me from error. I am grateful to Henry Howard for meticulous copy-editing. Any mistakes that survive are entirely my own.

Architectural history, like architecture, demands a certain amount of travel. This is not on the scale of the subject of this book, who must have spent as much time inside railway carriages as he did at home. Even so, my wife Naomi may feel a twinge of sympathy for Lutyens's abandoned Lady Emily during my enforced absences. For her patience and that of all my family, as well as for their endless support and encouragement, I am enormously grateful. None of them has become a Theosophist.

ONE

THE SURREY HILLS

Chinthurst Hill, Surrey 1893–95

Munstead Wood, Surrey 1896

'Aunt Bumps', as Lutyens irreverently dubbed Gertrude Jekyll. The caricature comes from a letter of about 1896 to his future wife Lady Emily Lytton.

O NE AFTERNOON IN THE 1880S, FORSTER ARBUTHNOT arrived in the Surrey village of Thursley, driving a carriage four-in-hand. He loved horses and wanted to commission a portrait of his favourite hack. A painter was said to live, with his large family, at a house called The Cottage. This was Charles Lutyens, an infantry captain who had served for some years in Canada, before becoming the regiment's musketry instructor at Aldershot. Musketry instruction was carried out in full dress, but that did not stop him, on one occasion, from leaping onto his horse and following the hunt when it passed by, leaving his companies to get on by themselves. Having a mathematical mind, according to a reminiscence by fellow officers after his death, he invented a stadiometer or rangefinder which remained in service with the army for nearly forty years.[1] But that was before he had become 'picturesque'. When Arbuthnot visited, the Lutyenses were found

> living rather like gypsies on the wildest part of Surrey's lovely heathland … A shock-haired boy and a lovely girl appeared when they perceived strangers approaching. There was no mistaking the man's vocation: artist was written in every line of his face and a certain look of inspiration glowed in his eyes.[2]

The shock-haired boy was Edwin Landseer Lutyens, who had been born in Onslow Square on March 29, 1869, the tenth boy in a family that would eventually number thirteen children.

Edwin's given names reflect Captain Lutyens's friendship with the animal painter Sir Edwin Landseer, darling of the 6th Duke and Duchess of Bedford (particularly the duchess, by whom he had children), who had cut such a dazzling figure as a twenty-four-year-old Royal Academician more than four decades earlier but was now mentally unstable and drinking heavily. If family tradition can be believed, Landseer wanted to adopt one of the boys – which would not have been so unusual then as it seems now, and the family home was certainly crowded – but Lutyens's mother Mary, an Irishwoman who had foregone her Roman Catholic upbringing to become an evangelical Protestant, vetoed the idea. She may have thought he had exercised enough influence over the family already. It was to follow Landseer's example that Charles left the army aged twenty-eight to become a painter. Alas, while Landseer had been in every artistic way brilliant in his early years, as well as feted socially, Charles possessed – for all his glow of inspiration – only moderate talent. An initial success did not last. Inherited money trickled into the sands. As the family slid into genteel poverty, he became increasingly eccentric, convinced that he had discovered the Venetian Secret – probably meaning the key to creating the colour effects of Bellini and Titian. We do not know because nobody was interested. He became bitter and obsessive. Meals were served on newspaper rather than tablecloth and consisted principally of cabbage. He spent as much time as he could hunting, his long white beard blowing in the wind.

Edwin's name did not long evoke unwelcome memories of Landseer, since he was known universally as Ned. The Cottage was first rented when he was seven. It was a second home, but one in which the family would spend a good part of the year, both during the summer (to escape dusty London) and the autumn and winter (for Charles's hunting). Farming had just entered the long depression that would dog British agriculture until the Second World War; but the landscape, easily reached by railway, was being viewed with new eyes. Heaths that Daniel Defoe had likened to Arabia Deserta in the 1720s could now, as we have seen, be called 'lovely'. Pinewoods and fast-draining, sandy soil seemed healthy to the tuberculosis-fearing Victorians. Charles Lutyens was not the only artist on the scene. The watercolourist Birket Foster and the poet laureate Alfred Tennyson built country houses in the 1860s; Helen Allingham arrived with her husband, the Irish poet William Allingham, at Sandhills, a hamlet south of Godalming, in 1881 and made Surrey's ramshackle cottages and farmhouses her principal subject: rosy cheeks among the rotting thatch (not that Surrey was a big county for thatch – some of it was made up). No less a figure than G.F. Watts – who had twice refused a baronetcy but accepted the Order of Merit – would come to Compton in 1891, building the Watts Gallery to perpetuate his work. The Lutyenses were on trend.

Where artists lead, the affluent middle classes follow, and writers who liked the old ways would soon be complaining of the cacophony of gramophones, tennis parties and motorcars. For the period of Lutyens's boyhood, however, the Surrey countryside remained in its prelapsarian condition, repository of what George Sturt, at nearby Farnham, would later call 'the home-made civilization of the rural English'.[3]

Growing up in the Surrey Hills shaped Lutyens. A walk around Thursley provides a foretaste of his early career. There is the ancient church of St Michael and All Angels, built of local Bargate stone, above whose crossing a central belfry was placed in the fifteenth century; internally, the massive oak cage that supports it is a spectacular example of medieval carpentry at its mightiest and most dramatic. Aged fourteen, Lutyens met the architect who came to restore it and, typically, gave him suggestions.[4] There are the cottages, in a medley of half-timbering and tile-hanging, plaster and brick, and with broad expanses of tiled roof, sometimes coming down in a catslide to shoulder height. There is the house opposite the church, whose Georgian brick façade cannot hide the fact that it is merely a front to an older timber-framed building with a hall – the asymmetrically placed front door standing where the screens passage would have been. There is the artistry of the Surrey vernacular, in techniques such as galleting, whereby masons pressed chips of flint into wide mortar joints (whether to reduce the amount of mortar, strengthen the wall or simply for visual effect is not clear). The Lutyenses' own home of The Cottage was a building of about 1800: Lutyens's early style would be peppered with details taken from the Georgian period to which it belonged.[5]

Lutyens absorbed all these things because he had to. Like his future hero, Sir Christopher Wren, he was poorly as a child, considered too delicate to play games or go to public school like his brothers – which must have relieved pressure on the straitened family finances; instead the most that could be managed was two years at a boarding school in Wandsworth. So he missed out on the rough and tumble of school days with his peer group, which left him feeling uneasy in the presence of men – hence the barrage of jokes and puns (not universally appreciated) which gave dinner companions a jaw-ache from laughing. But staying at home had compensations. Since, as he told Osbert Sitwell, long illness 'afforded me time to think …[I] had to teach myself, for my enjoyment, to use my eyes instead of my feet. My brothers hadn't the same advantage.'

Instead, he acquired an intimate knowledge of local buildings, internalised by means of a novel technique. Holding up a sheet of glass in front of the building he wanted to record, he needed only to make a few marks with a piece of sharpened soap to register the main shapes. Perhaps he needed to save paper; at any rate it was enough for him to commit the shapes to his exceptionally retentive memory. He would hang around Tickner's, the local carpenter's shop, or the builder's yard at Godalming, eight miles away, imbibing the principles of construction and the qualities of the materials used in it. The men may have talked to him about the practical application of mathematics: it is a subject of the craftsmen's manuals of the period. This may have quickened Lutyens's interest in the subject.[6]

One of the visitors to The Cottage was the sunny Randolph Caldecott, a former Manchester bank clerk turned illustrator, who now drove around the lanes in a dogcart with 'uproarious' company. He persuaded Mary and Charles that Ned should get some kind of education, recommending the National Art Training School, forerunner to the Royal College of Art, near Onslow Square in South Kensington. There Ned won the Queen's Prize for draughtsmanship but left after two years, without finishing the course. This young man in a hurry was already building wattle-and-daub barns for local farmers.

The god of all would-be architects in these years was Richard Norman Shaw. Shaw belonged to a generation for whom the intensely religious Gothic Revival had run its course; he and his contemporaries synthesised the tile-hanging and leaded lights, half-hipped gables and timber-framing that they saw in the countryside into a style that they called Old English. This was followed by the Queen Anne Revival, derived from the red-brick architecture of the seventeenth century flavoured with borrowings from Japan. At the end of the nineteenth century, Shaw introduced neo-Baroque to the capital, as a style that reflected the imperial pomp of the era. The young Ned actually met Shaw, who had been asked to design an extension to the Arbuthnots' country house. On seeing the sketch, he had no compunction in correcting it. 'With extraordinary dexterity … [he took] a pencil and with a stroke or two indicated where a great improvement could be made to the design.'[7] Shaw did not greatly care for the cheek but his interest was piqued. Lutyens oiled his hair so that it wouldn't stand up, borrowed a friend's clothes and the vicar's stiff Sunday boots, and limped off to see the architect. According to Violet Stuart-Wortley, he set forth what we would now call a sustainability agenda, 'suggesting that anything put up by man should harmonise with what nature dictates including mud encased wooden piles, roofs of heather which were resistant to the elements, warm in winter and cool in summer and conforming with the surroundings'. This was what he had learnt from farm buildings. To Shaw, it seemed fanciful at best. When it was time for Lutyens to find a position as a paying pupil in an architectural firm, it would not be in Shaw's office but that of Ernest George and Peto.

Later, Lutyens would say he was 'sent to an architect whose name I forget … After two days I ran away.' This may not have been meant quite seriously but nevertheless we may suspect Lutyens of myth-making. Christopher Hussey, who presumably talked to Lutyens about his early life, gives the impression that he was a largely untaught genius, a child of the Surrey lanes. The truth is that he stayed with Ernest George for eighteen months, not two days, and – for all his dismissive comments about architects who derived their inspiration from annual sketching tours on the Continent – learnt his own drawing style there. No doubt he would also have learnt a thing or two about the planning of large country houses. Lutyens might have liked Harold Peto, George's partner at the time – he replaced Thomas Vaughan, dead from 'brain fever' supposedly brought on by overwork; Peto became known as a poet among garden designers, evoking dreamy Italian moods. But as the son of a railway contractor, his role for George was to work up new clients, and Lutyens would not have known him. The office had a large practice, building red brick and terracotta, Flemish-gabled houses around Sloane Street and any number of country houses, often in the style that John Betjeman dubbed 'Jacobethan'.

While with George and Peto, Lutyens dazzled the partners' leading assistant, the Tonbridge-educated, cricket-playing Herbert Baker, who found that he 'quickly absorbed all that was best worth learning: he puzzled us at first, but we soon found that he seemed to know by intuition some great truths of our art which were not to be learned there.' But at the age of nineteen – and after what was certainly a short stay in the office – a legacy of £100 and a fee to design Crooksbury for a family friend enabled Lutyens to set up on his own; the more stolid Baker stuck it out for eight years.[8]

In 1891 Ned also encountered the work of Philip Webb, several of whose buildings were on the south slopes of the Surrey Hills.[9] He initially mistook the freshness for the work of youth, but instead came to realise that Webb was simply possessed of 'the eternal youth of genius, though it was conjoined with another attribute of genius – thoroughness.' Lutyens had probably seen Great Tangley Manor at Bramley. Originally Tudor, Great Tangley had suffered the fate of numerous manor houses during the Georgian period, when small dark rooms were out of fashion. According to *Country Life* – 'that elegant publication', wrote the ascetic Webb with scorn – the place had sunk into use 'as a farmhouse; the moat was choked with earth and rubbish, and overgrown with brambles and wild brushwood'.[10] Romantic owners kissed many such sleeping beauties back to life, while the rest mouldered and collapsed.

Unlike most of the other progressive architects of his generation, Lutyens is not recorded as having belonged to the Society for the Protection of Ancient Buildings, founded by Webb and William Morris in 1877 to prevent the despoliation of churches by overzealous restorers (the very fate which had befallen Thursley). But at Great Tangley he would have seen the results of its mantra: that old work should be left as far as possible as found, with new work being made to look unashamedly what it was – new.

The synthesis might be compared to the mix of styles we see in Lutyens's work, once he got into his stride. Not that Lutyens quite shared Webb's reverence towards existing architecture. In reply to Mark Fenwick, wondering what to do about the Victorian house he had just bought at Abbotswood, he advised: 'Blow it up, and start again.' He wanted to build, he *had* to build and he was completely confident in his own powers, even if things sometimes went wrong (as they were to do in a big way at Castle Drogo). This was another difference with the ascetic Webb, who was too fastidious to develop a big practice.

Lutyens's very first jobs consisted of modest alterations and additions around Thursley. No less a figure than the aesthete and sage John Ruskin advised Lutyens's contemporary (and later friend) Detmar Blow to abandon the idea of learning the practice of architecture from an established member of the profession: he ought instead to become a clerk of works and absorb the knowledge he would gain from working with craftsmen. While Lutyens did not have such an illustrious mentor, *faute de mieux* he began the same way. But within a remarkably short time the young man with the unruly hair and infectious sense of humour had charmed one or two wealthy individuals into entrusting him with major commissions.

Compared to the late start made by most architects, Lutyens's early entry into the profession made him something of a child prodigy, but he did not find his feet straight away. He was twenty-four when he received the commission to build Chinthurst Hill at Wonersh, for a lady doctor of decided views who had been on the point of marrying an earl. It is a jumble of Norman Shaw-derived features, without the bold controlling idea that typified Lutyens's later work. Fireplaces smoked and dust sheets were put on the windowsills whenever it rained to soak up the water that came through. The client lived there for only two years before moving with her new husband (not an earl) to the Isle of Mull. Later it was home to the architect Harry Goodhart-Rendel, whose widowed mother had been bought the house by his grandfather; coming there as a young boy, he loved its 'romantic complication':

> Odd rooms at odd levels; enormous stone ingle fireplaces; a gallery looking down over the staircase through casements of leaded horn; peculiar door latches; a wonderful burglar alarm on the back stairs where a board could be set at night to ring a bell if anyone trod upon it; a thrilling outside door, in an upper passage, that opened onto nothing, but through which luggage could be hoisted from the roof of a carriage below …

Such marvels were perhaps more appealing to children than grown-ups, and Lutyens played to his junior audience, designing a little window glazed with horn to allow them to peer down from upstairs when a party was on. Whimsies for the very young would become a stock in trade.

Home life at The Cottage was becoming increasingly odd but Lutyens remained close to his mother. Her influence was replaced as his life went on by other older women who provided the reassurance he needed and who helped him with his career. Barbara Webb, wife of the squire of nearby Milford, introduced him to his first clients. Then, in the summer that he opened his office, he went to a tea party in the Surrey Hills and met the dumpy and myopic spinster, Gertrude Jekyll. More than twenty years his senior, Miss Jekyll was a skilled craftswoman, who had turned to gardening as her eyesight deteriorated. Horticulturally, her mentor had been William Robinson, apostle of *The Wild Garden* (as he called one of his many publications) whose naturalistic style was revolutionary at a time of formal parterres planted in decorative patterns made by thousands of gaudy tender plants from the greenhouse. Aesthetic effect was everything for Jekyll, who had the eye of a painter; while she loved the simplicity of native plants, she combined them with exotics that she had seen on her travels around the Mediterranean and the Near East. In the act of reinventing the country house garden for her many clients across Britain, she needed an architect for her future home, Munstead Wood. Conversation between her and Ned did not flow, but as she was on the point of stepping onto her pony cart, she asked him to call on her the next day at Munstead House, outside Godalming. It was the beginning of an exceptional friendship.

Munstead Wood for the gardener Gertrude Jekyll, built from the local materials of Bargate stone, clay tile and oak. Jekyll rejoiced in the sound of bricks being laid, described as the 'ringing music of the soft-tempered blade cutting a well-burnt brick'.'

On first meeting her, Lutyens's future wife Lady Emily Lytton was thrilled. As she wrote to a literary friend:

> She is the most enchanting person and lives in the most fascinating cottage you ever saw. Mr Lutyens calls her Bumps, and it is a very good name. She is very fat and stumpy, dresses rather like a man, little tiny eyes, very nearly blind and big spectacles. She is simply fascinating.[11]

Photographs show that this pen portrait and Lutyens's own irreverent caricatures were not far from the truth; but Miss Jekyll had not always been forty-three. She had once looked elegant on a horse, as well as being an adventurous, not to say indomitable traveller – a friend sketched her in Rhodes in 'heavy marching order', weighed down by drawing impedimenta. Her parents' circle had been intellectual and artistic. The young Gertrude met Ruskin and attended the Kensington School of Art. George Leslie RA found her to be

> Clever and witty in conversation, active and energetic in mind and body … there is hardly any useful handicraft the mysteries of which she has not mastered – carving, modelling, house painting, carpentry, smith's work, repoussé work, gilding, wood-inlaying, embroidery, gardening and all manner of herb and culture.[12]

Gardening took centre stage when poor eyesight made fine work such as embroidery more difficult.

Unlike her friend Hercules Brabazon Brabazon, or 'Brabby' as Jekyll called him, a gentleman watercolourist who did not need to sell his work, she was an unmarried woman, well-connected but not rich, whose talents had to pay for her way of life. To this extent she was representative of a new phenomenon: the independent woman who worked for her living. A generation before, a spinster was likely to become a companion or a governess. Attitudes, however, were changing in the era of the suffragettes. Munstead Wood which was not only the place that she lived, in carefully curated surroundings, but her place of business. The brief for the house included a work room for the practice of craft, stored with woods for inlay, sheets of horn, bone and tortoiseshell, and collections of ornamental hinges, keys and handles; a book room where she wrote books and articles; a dark room where she developed the photographs that she took, often for publication; and a shop where flowers could be sold to the public. Not only did she design gardens but she supplied the plants for them from her own nursery. The house was just one incident in Jekyll's busy domestic world, much of which was spent outside. Work on the garden began more than ten years before that on the house. For her, the healthy soil of Munstead Wood was not a barren wasteland, as it might have appeared to William Cobbett on his Rural Rides of the 1820s, but ideal for the sort of plants she had seen on her travels around the Near East. She mixed native plants with exotics, grew clematis and roses through the silver birch trees of the woodland, and planted the scars left by old cart tracks with spring bulbs.

Jekyll, like Lutyens, had been born in London but her parents moved to Surrey when she was five. For a time the family trans-ferred to Berkshire – a period of exile, as Gertrude saw it – but after Captain Jekyll's death, Gertrude's brother Colonel Herbert Jekyll built Munstead House for them. The house was designed by J.J. Stevenson – Jaughty to his family, short for Naughty John due to his penchant for practical jokes.[13] In it Gertrude designed and built a fireplace, while Herbert, who enjoyed craft work in his time off from the army and civil service, carved decorations. But she knew that she would not continue to live there after her mother's death, which came in 1895 – hence Munstead Wood. Before this, however, came cottagey Munstead Hut – 'tiny,' as Jekyll described

The garden at Munstead Wood provided Jekyll with endless subjects for photography. She took and developed photographs herself, using them to illustrate her numerous books and articles. This is one of Jekyll's Autochromes, an early colour process patented in 1903.

Exuberant vernacular. Lutyens took inspiration from the old buildings that he and Jekyll saw on expeditions around the Surrey lanes but used them in excitingly new ways. This photograph shows Bargate stone combined with clay tile and oak.

it in *Home and Garden*; a composition of low eaves, dormers and tile-hanging, with two tall chimneys as the only bravura touch. It would be a staging post from which she could watch the larger house being built.

Jekyll had strong views about domestic living but not the ability to realise them in three dimensions. For this she needed a pliable architect and decided to make Lutyens – young, gangly and hilarious – her tool. She shaped him. Together the oddly assorted couple explored local villages, exclaiming delightedly on the buildings. Here was a hand-made world of farmer's smocks and sugar-nippers, wicker bird cages and horse accoutrements – old-fashioned artefacts that she collected as they went out of use. It was an education in the Arts and Crafts, which the quick-witted young man soon absorbed. Here was 'the promise of a new exhilarating sphere of invention'.[14]

A sketchbook in the RIBA collection records Lutyens's first thoughts for Munstead Wood. They are charming examples of the Ernest George style, but did not meet with approval; the composition was too grand and the interiors were practically Baronial. There would be many battles between architect and client, which – in a useful lesson for a young architect – the client usually won.[15] Her desire was above all for simplicity, of a kind that would have puzzled her stiff-backed contemporaries. No drive came up through the garden: from the lane, visitors entered by a wooden gate and must walk the remaining yards to the house.

Strangely, Jekyll's own early thoughts for Munstead Wood involved marble. It was Ruskin himself who corrected her, writing in a letter that white walls and tapestries set the proper note for a house in a northern clime. By the time the design was finished, the elements were nothing if not local: rough Bargate stone, tawny-coloured and impossible to square; clay tile roofs; oak frames to the doors and windows, with iron latches; brick and half-timber in places. There were famously deep gables and sheltered spots for conversation.

The vernacular themes were already being filtered through Lutyens's architectural imagination. Like any architect of the day, he set out his façades using the tools available, principally T-square, set square and compass; so even the apparently vernacular elevations conform to basic principles of geometry. Squares and circles (in the form of old millstones) are seen in the garden too. The sense of geometry is increased by the unbroken planes of the façades: it was a characteristic of the Surrey vernacular, seen in the photographs of *Old West Surrey* – Jekyll's requiem to the beloved land of her youth – that window frames are set flush with the wall (although protected at Munstead Wood by slightly projecting rows of clay tile). The doorway to the shop is combined with a window, under a single lintel – an idea that was Lutyens's own. In the gable above, at Jekyll's command, is a small opening, now a glazed window but originally left open, to allow owls to roost in the attic.

No Lutyens house, whatever the style, reveals itself in an obvious and straightforward manner: visitors must go on a journey, which adds to the drama as well as to the apparent extent of buildings that were not always big. This was as true for Munstead Wood as anywhere else. Visitors who opened the modest wooden gate from the lane saw first, across the lawn, nothing but an arch in a screen wall; from the arch radiated bands of tile as though in a sunburst, a motif that became practically a signature of Lutyens's garden architecture. Once through the arch, it was necessary to turn through ninety degrees beneath a dramatically over-structured oak frame; here at last was the front door. The twists and turns in Lutyens's plans make often relatively small houses seem larger, by heightening the sense of exploration.

The main room at Munstead Wood is the hall. It betrays Lutyens's inexperience. Munstead Hut, which Jekyll occupied while

Entry to Lutyens's houses is always a journey. At Munstead Wood, visitors had to cross a lawn, go through an arch and turn a right angle before reaching this door. The overscale timber framing resembles a fragment of a previous building.

Munstead Wood was building and later used as a place for writing in, has a staircase next to the fireplace; but such a cottagey arrangement is not suitable in the hall of the much larger house. Moreover, because the combination of a wide room with a low ceiling created a rather dull space, Lutyens introduced timber braces at the sides, which have no functional purpose. This was anathema to Arts and Crafts doctrine. But the deficiencies may not have troubled Jekyll who spent all day out of doors, only coming in after sunset to rest in her favourite chair in front of the fire – as William Nicholson found when he came to paint the portrait that is now in the National Portrait Gallery. (It was while waiting for her to come in that he painted her no-nonsense boots.) The glory of the house lies in the broad first-floor gallery, its walls lined with oak panelling and display cases for Jekyll's collections, the powerful oak beams overhead

The first-floor gallery. Jekyll could remember the oak trees, which had been growing nearby, before they had been cut down and seasoned in the timber merchant's yard.

suggesting a forest. It was so successful that Lutyens reproduced it at Deanery Garden, the house in Berkshire which he built for Edward Hudson, founder of *Country Life*.

Working together on Munstead Wood, Jekyll and Lutyens came to be in such sympathy that they created a special magic they could sell to other people. By 1900 they had designed twenty-seven gardens together; in the course of their informal partnership, which only ended a few years before Jekyll's death at Munstead in 1932, the number had reached over one hundred. Their areas of responsibility remained as they had been at Munstead: Jekyll orchestrated the planting, Lutyens designed the garden architecture. The result is described by the garden historian Jane Brown:

> On the whole these gardens were traditional – their design was dictated by the geometry of the house, the materials of the houses (sandstone and brick) were extended to make terraces and paths which were softened with bergenias, *Stachys lanata* and santolina; there were always dry stone retaining walls dripping with lavenders, pinks and valerian, clipped yew as a background for clumps of yuccas, swathes of pink lilies and hollyhocks, steely blue echinops and cloudy gypsophila, and substantial pergolas, vine and rose-covered, in direct reply to Robinson's scorn of rustic work.

These were artists' gardens. To many people they remain the ideal of the English garden, even though Jekyll's palette included many exotic or otherwise non-native plants.

Some of Jekyll's wide circle of garden-loving friends wanted houses. It was through Miss Jekyll that Lutyens, still very much a country boy, met Princess Louise, a daughter of Queen Victoria, and got the commission to convert the Ferry Inn at Rosneath, in Argyll, Scotland, into a place she could stay. Miss Jekyll also saw to it that Sir William and Lady Chance, who first spotted her perched on a ladder outside Munstead Wood giving directions to workmen, should dismiss Halsey Ricardo, who had already prepared the foundations of their new country house, Orchards, and replace him with Lutyens. (It was not the sort of thing to make Lutyens popular in the profession.) Soon after, it seemed natural that Miss Jekyll's brother, now Colonel Sir Herbert Jekyll, when he was Commissioner for the British Section of the International Exhibition to be held in Paris in 1900, should ask Lutyens to design the British Pavilion. Modelled on the Hall at Bradford-on-Avon, it was a temporary building but seen by thousands of people.

The next year, 1901, Miss Jekyll introduced Ned, as she and everyone else called him, to Mark Fenwick of Abbotswood, and later probably also to Ernest Blackburn, the skilful amateur gardener who built Little Thakeham. Her extended family was also the source of many commissions. Pamela and Barbara, daughters of her brother Herbert, both married Liberal MPs (Reginald McKenna and the Hon. Francis McLaren) who needed townhouses, as did Barbara's sister-in-law Priscilla (married to Sir Henry Norman). 'Reginald McKenna has bought a site in London and I do hope he asks me to build for him,' Lutyens wrote of 36 Smith Square. 'Pamela is for me – and the whole Jekyll family.' For McKenna, this was only the beginning: he went on to commission two country houses and, as Chairman of the Midland Bank, four bank buildings. Herbert's sister-in-law was Frances Horner at Mells Manor in Somerset; the Horners were not flush with money but inspired Lutyens to design one of his most moving testaments to the First World War, the equestrian monument to their son Edward in Mells church.

That lay in the future. For the time being perhaps Jekyll's biggest favour was to introduce Ned to Edward Hudson, whose magazine,

Country Life was founded in 1897. That year, though, would be important to Lutyens for another reason. During it Lutyens married a girl whom he had met at a party, looking so unhappy that he longed to rescue her with his jokes. Her name was Lady Emily Lytton.

TWO

OH EMY
IT'S SPLENDID

Le Bois des Moutiers, Normandy 1898

Knebworth House, Hertfordshire (garden and decoration) 1901

Homewood, Hertfordshire 1901

Les Communes, Normandy 1909

Knebworth Garden Village, Hertfordshire, 1904–1912

Tyringham Hall Garden and Pavilions, Buckinghamshire 1924–8

The architect as knight errant. Another of Lutyens's drawings shows him, with T-square, kneeling before his future wife Lady Emily Lytton, depicted as a queen empress in the diamond jubilee year of 1897. 'I have no great city for you to reign over,' he wrote, 'but with such little as I have I worship you and pay homage to my queen … Oh Emy it's splendid.'

T O BE A GREAT ARCHITECT REQUIRES MORE THAN introductions to potential clients, who must be charmed or cajoled into providing opportunities to build; more even than innate genius. It also demands the drive to pursue commissions at all costs, supported by the stamina to see them through. Lutyens was never too busy to take on more work. He could not afford to be: he had got married. In other respects, Lutyens's bride did not greatly affect his architecture – in fact she took little interest in it. That did not lessen Lutyens's devotion to her. The coat of arms that Lutyens adopted on becoming a Knight Commander of the British Empire in 1930 includes a crest formed of two concentric circles of twisted silk on which are three five-pointed stars; if the circles were a clock face, the stars would stand at four o'clock, eight o'clock and twelve o'clock – I am grateful to Mark Lutyens for suggesting that this could refer to his marriage, which took place on August 4 at midday.[1] Even so, Lady Emily principally enters this story as the recipient of the four thousand letters in the RIBA Drawings Collection which are the best source of information on Lutyens's life, architecture and thoughts: no other architect has left such a spontaneously vivid record.

For Lutyens, the first meeting with Emily had been electric. She was tall, large-nosed and spiritual. The granddaughter of the raffish Edward Bulwer-Lytton, politician and man of letters, Emily grew up at Knebworth House in Hertfordshire; her father, the 1st Earl of Lytton, had been viceroy of India. The family was high octane but not rich by the standards of their class. One sister was a staunch Conservative, who was married to a brother of the future prime minister, Balfour; another was to become a prominent suffragette. Lutyens may have seen in this a more exalted echo of his own embarrassing family – but in terms of experience of the world, Emily was in a different league. For the four years before her father's death in 1891, she had lived with him in Paris, where he was the British ambassador. On her return to England, the Arabist and lothario Wilfrid Scawen Blunt, thirty-five years her senior, had pursued her with dishonourable intent. She had an emotional void to fill. Lutyens – 'mad but so nice,' as she called him[2] – must have seemed a quirky choice of life partner, and not surprisingly, her mother strongly disapproved of the match.

Lutyens's courtship was profoundly romantic. He worshipped her, oblivious to the marked differences in their personalities. The couple had to wait until the young architect could show he was earning enough for them to marry. Meanwhile, the tongue-tied Lutyens expressed his romantic devotion to his beloved by design-ing a little casket covered in green leather, full of symbols of their future life together: an anchor signifying hope, a brass pipe stopper (Lutyens always had a pipe in his mouth and several others in his pocket: the stopper evoked the pipes that would be smoked by the domestic hearth), a heart, a crucifix, a tiny Bible accompanied by a magnifying glass and so on. Among them was a sketch for the house that he hoped they would build. It was to have been gleaming white. In letters he would doodle pictures of himself as a knight errant, carrying a T-square. To Emily's mother, Lady Lytton, on the other hand, married life was not all a matter of green leather caskets. Eventually, though, he got on the right side of her: only a few years would pass before she was living in Homewood, the ingenious small house he had designed for her – wittily in the form of a classical house that seems to have been engulfed by a vernacular one (the opposite from the way houses develop historically). As ever, Lutyens turned the entrance into a journey. The Baroque doorcase gives into an unpromising passage, and only when the visitor performs a right-angled turn and enters the hall and drawing room on the south-west front does the garden reveal itself. Drama is given to the stair by the bank of hidden windows – like the weavers' windows that serve the workspaces in Georgian attics – that light it from above. But in arranging the marriage settlement Lady Lytton was firm: he would have to take out an expensive insurance bond, which would provide for Emily if he should die. That and the need to maintain a domestic establishment appropriate to a countess's daughter – devoted to the spirit life but unable to manage without a large staff of servants – made Lutyens permanently anxious about money. He was the architect who could not say no.

The marriage finally took place in the church in front of the Lyttons' country house, Knebworth, in 1897. They spent their honeymoon in Holland, where even now a hint of future differences emerged on the beach at Scheveningen. She liked looking at the sea; Lutyens hated it, and sat next to her, his chair facing the other way, firmly towards the land. Already she found her husband's sexual demands selfish and physically painful, and she would dislike everything about giving birth to their five children. In London, he was distressed by her inability to keep house. The man who became Britain's leading domestic architect never achieved the kind of setting he provided for so many clients – whose establishments he would privately castigate if he found them 'uncomfy'.[3] There would be no dream house in gleaming white. Home life was bleak. He was in any case constantly away from the domestic sphere, making site visits and schmoozing clients. The legacy for posterity is the large number of letters that went between the couple, because they were so often separated.

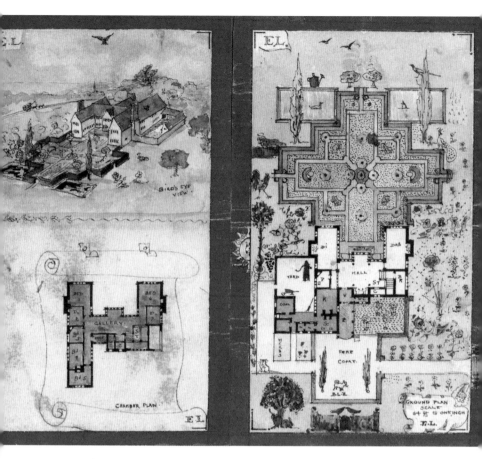

Lutyens designed a casket for Lady Emily before their engagement. Red lacquered with tooled gold on ball feet, the casket was filled with 'treasures' including a roll of plans for a 'white house', which Lutyens envisaged to be their future home.

One consequence of the marriage for Lutyens's career was a host of projects at Knebworth. Although Emily's father had been made an earl, the state of the Lyttons' finances meant that their country house was often let out; this was a common practice among cash-strapped aristocrats who could not afford to keep up their seats and may, in any case, have preferred a sociable life in London to the rigours of existence in an unmodernised pile. Besides, when the 1st Earl Lytton had died in 1891, his son

Victor, the 2nd Earl, was fifteen and had no need for a country house. By 1904, however, Victor saw a new form of revenue for the estate in developing a Garden Village; no doubt influenced by the example of Letchworth Garden City, fifteen miles to the north. Not that his first thought was to enlist Lutyens's help: Ned had to remind him of his existence by writing: 'Your buildings proposed are horrible and very vulgar to look upon – do you mind this?' The project was long in gestation. By the time the brochure had been printed in about 1911, it could be announced that Lutyens had prepared a 'comprehensive scheme' for the development of a thousand acres, in conjunction with the planner Thomas Adams who had run Letchworth from 1903 to 1906. The plan owed more to the formal principles of Letchworth than the faux rusticity of Hampstead Garden Suburb, where it was Lutyens who contributed the only classically composed space: Central Square. Knebworth's existing medieval lanes and the scatter of houses, many for railway workers, which had sprung up around the railway station of 1884, were subsumed into a geometrical pattern of straight, perhaps tree-lined roads. The new homes were to be set behind verges, hedges and generous front gardens. Four segments were built before the First World War brought the initial phase of development to a halt, leaving some of the unbuilt land to be occupied, decades later, by suburban infill, somewhat compromising the vision. Beyond the plan, Lutyens contributed a golf clubhouse, in a countrified early Georgian style, a twist being provided by a very deep roof with dormers and cupola; and the church of St Martin – a Greek cross within a square, very plain inside but majestic from the use of two sizes of order, one for the arcades, the other at the crossing. Rural though Knebworth Garden Village may have been, it was one of Lutyens's few exercises in town planning before Delhi, where – on a greatly inflated scale – the principles are surprisingly similar.

Plan of Knebworth Garden Village. Lutyens not only purged Knebworth House of some of its Victorian ornament but was consulting architect to his brother-in-law's new garden village. It was one of only two town planning ventures before he laid out New Delhi.

Since Victor's marriage in 1902 to the beautiful, lively Pamela Chichele Plowden, Lutyens had been helping his new sister-in-law to bring Knebworth House into the twentieth century. Consisting of only one wing of the original Tudor quadrangle, Knebworth had been romanticised by Elizabeth Bulwer-Lytton, who settled there in 1811, and her son, the poet, novelist and philosopher Edward Bulwer-Lytton, who gave it a fantastical skyline of barley-sugar chimneys, heraldic beasts and gargoyles. Lutyens culled the romantic excess, too heady for neo-Georgian taste or his own preference for aesthetic discipline. The geometrical flowerbeds of the parterre were removed – their outline can still be seen during dry summers – and lawn and pleached limes put in their place. Some of the plethora of mythological figures in white marble were placed in niches in a tall hedge; the stucco beasts on the parapet were taken down. Inside the house, ceilings with pendants were replaced with copies of examples in the Victoria and Albert Museum. Silk hangings, suspended from poles, replaced Spanish leather. Dark panelling was 'pickled', making it lighter, or removed in favour of white plaster. The suits of armour went from the great hall. The journey from Bulwer-Lytton's study to his bedroom involved crossing the Picture Gallery, possibly full of guests; if he was in his dressing gown he would have the butler announce that he was officially invisible. Lutyens provided the Red Passage to save the 2nd Earl this embarrassment. Lutyens probably also had a hand in the rearrangement of the bedroom floors. He certainly designed the light fitting in the nursery, ringed by angels whose silhouette is projected onto the ceiling at night.

Once Lutyens was married to Emily, the Lytton family did what they could. Emily's aunt Elizabeth Loch thought he should design the South Kensington Museum and, after a visit to South Africa, raised the prospect of 'Africa's Cathedral' – but these were dreams. More prosaically, he was asked to add a billiard room, service wing and bedrooms to the Lochs' country house in Suffolk, Stoke

College. For Emily's sister Betty and her husband, Gerald Balfour, soon to be President of the Board of Trade, he built a somewhat charmless brick house called Fisher's Hill on Hook Heath, near Woking (Betty's close friend, the composer and suffragette Dame Ethel Smyth, came to live nearby and gleefully recounted practising stone throwing by night with Emmeline Pankhurst on the heath). But while Lutyens's aristocratic marriage helped him rise in society, the Lytton connection did not gain him many new clients outside the family – with one notable exception. Another of Emily's aunts, the garden writer and vegetarian Theresa Earle, knew a Frenchman whose niece had married a French Protestant banker with English tastes called Guillaume Mallet. Mallet wanted his seaside house in Varengeville to be remodelled and it was perhaps through Mrs Earle that he found Lutyens – although he had already begun to acquire a profile in France from his commission to design the British Pavilion at the Paris Exhibition of 1900. Mallet had been sent to stay in England during the Franco-Prussian War of 1870; the experience awakened his passion for gardens. Returning to France he entered the French cavalry but resigned his commission in 1896, at the time of the Dreyfus affair. This left him free to turn his Varengeville property into a work of architectural poetry, where he could live surrounded by music, with a garden that sloped to the sea like those he had seen in Cornwall; 'Aunt Bumps' would draw plans for the garden in 1904. Art mingled with the ozone of the air, and when Jean Cocteau visited the house with André Gide in 1913, he wrote a poem. What was the meaning of the rippling, many-faceted windows over the porch? The panes of glass, unusually small, glinted like a cut diamond in the sun.

From its Hispanic decoration, the existing dwelling was known as The Mexican House. Lutyens smothered it in roughcast and tile-hanging. His principal addition contains a two-storey music room. It has its own roof line, with one of the eaves sweeping down low on the garden front. Light dances in through a tall, south-facing window with wooden mullions which zigzag in and out. Some of the panes in the mullions open to prevent the room becoming too hot. If music, played at the grand piano, provided the principal purpose of the room, it probably also functioned as the sort of multipurpose space known as a living hall. Less paternalistic than the Victorian great hall, living halls provided a place for people to talk, read newspapers and kill time, as well as make music. The fascinating window gives a view down the sloping lawn to the Woodland Garden beyond which are glimpses of the sea; ships seem to sail between the tops of the tall trees.

Lutyens returned to Varengeville a decade later to build a second house for the Mallets, Les Communes – of red brick and to the kind

The serene double-height music room at Le Bois des Moutiers, in Normandy. The oak mullions of the window zig-zag in and out: inside the light seems to dance on the walls and ceiling and outside the glass glitters when catching the sun. Individual panes can be opened for ventilation.

of butterfly plan that was often favoured at the seaside, presumably because it trapped the sun. 'O, I don't want to stay with the Mallets, it is so uncomfy', Lutyens wailed to his wife. For all the chaos of his own childhood home, he hated houses that were badly run or inadequately provided. However beautiful, the way of life at Le Bois des Moutiers was also Spartan – too much so even for Lutyens, who had little feeling for padded comfort and loved the romantic severity of Lindisfarne Castle. But that was not the only drawback of the house. Another could be found in a cupboard – always kept locked – in the living hall. It contained their library of Theosophical books. For the Mallets were not only lovers of beauty, music and gardens, but leading members of the Theosophical Society, the spiritual organisation founded by Helena Blavatsky in 1875 and popularised by Mrs Annie Besant. It was run by, and appealed particularly to, women. Emily entered Mrs Besant's intimate circle.

In the summer of 1911, she took all her five children to Varengeville where they stayed in two farmhouses. The Mallets had invited two Indian boys, Jiddu Krishnamurti and his brother Nitya, to stay at Les Communes. The former had been identified by the Theosophists as the next World Teacher, a figure who it was thought emerged every two thousand years to show mankind the way; the last manifestation had been Jesus Christ. Emily, who had already been enraptured by them in London, devotedly spent the mornings at Les Communes, taking part in Shakespeare readings. For the first time she fell passionately, if probably sexlessly in love.

Lutyens had much to suffer. At home, Emily not only adopted a vegetarian regime for herself but for the children, then toddlers. Lutyens stolidly remained the only meat-eater in the household. In another letter he had to admit: 'Architecture takes me away from you in some ways.' Literally, that was true of his punishing round of site visits; but architecture was also a country of the spirit to which Emily had no passport.

Profundity, for Lutyens, meant the pair of pavilions – one for bathing, one a Temple of Music – that he designed for the gardens of Tyringham Hall in Buckinghamshire, in the mid 1920s. He liked to sit in the Temple of Music alone, in communion with the faultless geometry he had created. Was it a coincidence that the clients – the American banker Frederick Konig, and his wife, Baroness Gerda von Chappuis – were Theosophists? Here, for once, Ned's deepest spiritual instincts coincided with those of Emily's world.

Interior of the Temple of Music at Tyringham. The client's wife, Mrs Konig, was a great lover of music. Lutyens set the organ pipes below the ground so that the music would waft gently through the elaborate metal grilles set within the floor.

THREE

BOOM IT LIKE ANYTHING

Deanery Garden, Berkshire 1901

Lindisfarne Castle, Northumberland 1903

Plumpton Place, East Sussex 1927

Edward Hudson, proprietor of *Country Life*, the young Barbara Lutyens and Lutyens going to their bedrooms in Hudson's Lindisfarne Castle, on Holy Island, off the coast of Northumberland. Spatially it was a thrilling house, but not comfortable.

'**D**O GET *COUNTRY LIFE* THIS WEEK,' LUTYENS WROTE to his wife in 1911. 'There is Temple Dinsley in it, and some baths mantels etc. in the supplement by me.' Then the same year: 'Riddle [sic] Hudson etc. want me to prepare anonymously a King Edward Memorial scheme at once and they are going to boom it like anything.' More than most architects, Lutyens had a modern understanding of the importance of PR. His main organ of publicity was *Country Life*.

Founded in 1897, *Country Life* could easily have been mistaken for a bastion of tradition – and in some ways it was. But it also advocated a new taste and way of living, which combined a love of old furniture and time-worn materials with artistic gardening and a nostalgia for the disappearing crafts of the countryside. This was not a magazine for professionals, such as *The Builder* or the *Architectural Review*; but to a savvy architect that was a strong part of its appeal – it was read by potential clients. While not ostensibly peddling an arty line, like *The Studio*, it had an aesthetic agenda, shaped by its proprietor Edward Hudson, whose eye was in turn guided by a small coterie of talented advisors, including Jekyll and, before long, Lutyens. The architecture and collections of the country house were seen as works of culture and beauty – which was novel at a time when some owners prided themselves on being anti-intellectual and philistine.

Part of the appeal of *Country Life* was its photographs, printed by a new American method of half-tone reproduction. This was an example of the technology that was rapidly transforming British life, not least in Lutyens's special sphere of interest at this time, the country house. Rooms could now be lit by electricity, requiring both housing for generators and a design novelty, the electric light fitting, although bulbs were so dim that they did not require shades. Steam was circulated through radiators to take off the chill – another aesthetic challenge: at Great Dixter, Lutyens hid them inside Tudor chests. Tin bathtubs were no longer carried in and out of bedrooms to be filled from kettles: water streamed into them from hot and cold bath taps.

Or owners could take showers, if they preferred, perhaps in an apparatus that bombarded them with water from different angles in a range of jet sizes. House telephones provided a more efficient means of summoning servants than the bell pull. The British Portable Vacuum Cleaner could be operated single-handedly by a maid: its ad shows an astonished footman looking on, relieved that he no longer has to carry out the rugs for beating, unaware that such inventions will soon make his job redundant. After the First World War, the mainstay of the advertising pages became the property market, as owners rushed to offload the country houses they could no longer afford to maintain; before 1914, unneeded country houses were usually rented rather than sold, but still advertised.

Although Lutyens's style celebrated the Arts and Crafts values of hand work and took its inspiration from the past, his clients did not eschew innovation. The south front of Fulbrook House may reimagine a timber-framed Wealden hall house of the late Middle Ages, but the Streatfields who owned it – they were among some of Lutyens's favourite clients – loved motoring. According to *The Car Illustrated*, Mrs Streatfield could strip down the engine of her Locomobile herself when helped by a lad from the village. Motor cars and all that pertained to them were a big subject for *Country Life*. The enthusiasm of both the magazine and Lutyens's clients (except for Bumps) ran counter to the general opinion of the countryside. For motoring was regarded as a plutocratic activity, and the bombastic Mr Toad parodied an all-too-recognisable type behind the wheel of the new glossy and expensive machines – apt to run over dogs, frighten horses and turn canary-coloured caravans into the ditch. Hostesses feared the revolution that would be caused if guests, instead of staying for a week, or even a few months, at a time, were able to hurry off to someone else's dinner table after luncheon. But Lutyens and *Country Life* were purveying a dreamily nostalgic world for people who were not so much dreamy or nostalgic as progressive. To borrow words from Scott Fitzgerald, they had 'the ability to hold two opposed ideas in the mind at the same time, and still retain the ability to function'.[1] The life served by Lutyens's early country houses – their scale, their plans, their room types and gardens – were thrillingly new. His use of the media to promote his career was a sign of how thoroughly Lutyens understood the twentieth century.

Towards the end of his life, Hudson – a Londoner by birth – described the origins of the magazine to Noel Carrington, brother of the Bloomsbury Group painter Dora Carrington and the book editor who ran Country Life Books:

> I was set on illustrating the magnificent houses I had seen up and down the country though at that time I had never had the chance to see the inside of any of them. You see, I was travelling for our printing firm, to get orders of course, but whenever I had the chance I took a bicycle with me on the train to see what I could of the houses from the outside. I believed that if I could illustrate them and their contents I had a magnificent subject for a paper. That's really how I started.[2]

A bachelor until the final years of his life, he did not shoot or hunt. He liked gardens, playing the cello and golf.

'Huddy' was even shyer than Ned and utterly lacking in glamour. But in spongebag trousers and watch chain, he would enter the *Country Life* offices like a whirlwind. Staff who had temporarily put their feet on the table – on press days, they might not go home before midnight – took them down again. Bells rang; pages that were typeset by the compositors in the attics of the building and printed by presses in the basement were rushed into his presence: each one was personally approved by the proprietor.[3] And beneath the bloodhound expression and dreary exterior beat a romantic heart. At one level this can be seen in his *grand amour* for the fiery Portuguese cellist Guilhermina Suggia for whom he bought a Montagnana cello of 1717; Suggia knew a good thing when she found it and she and Hudson were briefly engaged. It was also expressed in *Country Life*'s aesthetic presentation of ancient houses set amid noble parks, an approach alien to most aristocratic owners other than the elite, intellectual and arty group known as The Souls. 'All his life he searched for beauty for himself and his beloved *Country Life*,' wrote 'A Friend' (possibly Lutyens) in the obituary columns of *The Times* after his death; 'and this quest he pursued like a hunter, alert, groping, discarding, and finding.' Treasured projects, such as *The Dictionary of English Furniture* of the 1920s, never recovered their costs, although the reputation they established was beyond price.

Hudson, who never wrote in the magazine himself, had an outstanding gift for picking the right people. His first triumph was to recruit Gertrude Jekyll; Henry Avray Tipping followed in 1907. Previously a contributor to *The Garden*, which had been absorbed by *Country Life* two years before, he brought a new level of scholarship to the country house articles. Son of a railway director and MP, Tipping had skin in the game, as the owner, successively, of three idyllic houses in Wales which he romantically renovated and gardened. His diary for 1908 – a tiny volume but all that survives from his papers, which he ordered to be destroyed at his death – reveals him touring the country in Hudson's Rolls-Royce, with the chauffeur Perkins trying to avoid getting bogged down in the mud that was one of the perils of country roads. Furniture at *Country Life* became the preserve of the theatre designer and connoisseur Percy Macquoid, one of the first scholarly writers on old furniture. When, in 1909, Lawrence Weaver, the traveller for an ironmongery firm, published *English Leadwork: Its Art and History*, Hudson took note and brought him onto the staff. His special subject was the Small Country House, which would be the subject of numerous articles gathered together in a series of five volumes by Country Life Books. These homes were not so small by today's standards but nevertheless represented a new building type in the early twentieth century, intended to accommodate the barristers, retired colonial officials, senior civil servants and city types of the recently emerged upper middle class.

Jekyll introduced Hudson to Lutyens in about 1899. The architect regarded Hudson variously as a 'brick' and an 'angel'; to Hudson, Lutyens was quite simply a genius and he took every opportunity of promoting his cause. This began, practically on first meeting, with the commission to build Deanery Garden, on the site of an orchard in the Berkshire town of Sonning. Lutyens kept the ancient wall to the street, with the result that nothing can be seen of the house except for the complex roofscape. Privacy was valued by the Edwardians. Entrance is by a rather small doorway: Lutyens was a tall man but many of his doorways are low, creating a sense of *Alice in Wonderland* adventure to those who go through them. There is a fairytale sense of the unexpected, too, in the way that the house then unfolds. First comes a vaulted space, white chalk and striped with bands of tile – a piece of drama on an intimate scale for which nothing has prepared us. To the right appears a courtyard made of brick and timber-frame, somewhat like a cloister in feel (suggested by the clerical associations of the name, perhaps). But the door is opposite, and the vaulting continues inside, in a passage that leads to an oak staircase like that at Munstead Wood. The principal living spaces are a hymn to oak, thrown into prominence by walls of a monastic white. The monkish ambience may have suited Hudson, who was an early collector of antique furniture – oak and walnut being preferred to mahogany. As photographed for *Country Life*, the effect is beautiful but austere. A view that was not published in the magazine shows the dining room, its built-in dresser loaded with seventeenth-century pewter; the plain rush-seated chairs have no cushions. In the garden, Jekyll's painterly effects revealed 'the hand of the artist'. But for all the aesthetic care and appearance of timelessness, the house was judged 'a superb instance of what can be accomplished in a very short space of time,' the whole having

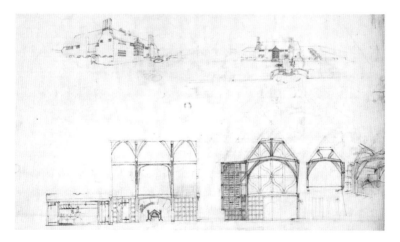

Deanery Garden, in the Berkshire town of Sonning, was a rhapsody in hand-made brick and oak, the perfect setting for Hudson's antique furniture. *Country Life* published it as 'the house of a man with a hobby – viz., rose-growing and wall-gardening'.

been brought to a state of perfection within only three years. Just because the house looked mellow and beautifully weathered did not mean that clients had to wait a long time for it.

Another country-house adventure began on August 12, 1901, when Hudson took Lutyens to dinner at his club. Writing to Emily the next day, Lutyens reported the astonishing outcome of Hudson's Northumberland holiday: he 'has offered for a castle!! on Holy Island – a real castle, & out of which he would have to turn if the Country went to war!' Beneath these words he scrawled, 'too funny.'

Perched on a conical outcrop of rock called Beblowe Crag, the castle had never been more than a fort, or gun emplacement, built in the Tudor period to protect a harbour that had become an important naval base in operations against Scotland, using stones pillaged from Lindisfarne Priory. In comparison to Bamburgh Castle, a few miles down the coast, bought by the plutocratic armaments manufacturer Lord Armstrong in the previous decade, it was small and almost comically inconvenient. There had never been any grand rooms. For centuries, the castle had been considered to be of such little strategic value that it was barely manned. In 1893 the garrison left it to the occasional use of the Coast Guard.

To many people, it might have been highly impractical, having nowhere to build the service courts and bedroom wings needed to entertain a large house party. But Lutyens, like Hudson, loved it. 'Ramparts and three miles from land!' he wrote excitedly – if not with geographical accuracy – after first hearing Hudson describe the place. In May 1904, Lutyens took the train down with a raven (because every castle should have one), whose 'beak makes a noise like castanettes'. With him was Gertrude Jekyll. Together they rumbled over the ridge-and-furrow fields in a wagonette, before crossing the haunting, seaweedy, rain-swept landscape of the sands. The fort was cold and the chimneys smoked, but it improved the next day, and Lutyens hurried out to hoist the flag. On the flat land a few

Lindisfarne Castle, on its crag. Lutyens carved some rooms out of the dense fabric of the old artillery fort and added others in the range beneath the pitched roof shown here.

minutes' walk from the castle Jekyll created a tiny cutting garden, protected by tall walls against the wind and sea spray.

In August 1906, as Emily recovered from the birth of their daughter Elisabeth, the future composer, Ned took the three youngster children to Lindisfarne, playing dominoes and Happy Families on the train. This was in advance of a ten week visit by Emily, for which the arrangements were not wholly faultless: 'Hudson & I sleep in the upper gallery upper bedroom, Barbie & Robert in the gun room, Nannie & Ursula next to it, Marbel in the Corner room. We shall have to move her & get two more beds. Hudson,' he added characteristically, 'forgot to order them.' More guests were expected, including Lord Riddell. A Major Crawford, who could not be squeezed into the castle, would have to sleep at the inn. It was 'such

Lutyens built three country houses for Hudson, all of them works of art in different ways. This photograph shows Lutyens's daughter Barbara playing with a toy town, in a photograph by the *Country Life* photographer Charles Latham in the style of Vermeer. It was taken in the kitchen at Lindisfarne.

joy to think the place is a success.' In the course of the summer, the *Country Life* photographer Charles Latham captured the Lutyens children in photographs lit like a Vermeer – the ultimate statement of Hudson's aesthetic. Needless to say, Lutyens could not resist supplementing the front door with a working portcullis. The exposed pinkish stone and slate floors in the entrance hall set the tone for the castle, although MacDonald Gill's wind indicator (there is rarely a shortage of wind on the island) introduces a decorative note. It depicts the 'invincible armada' being blown to pieces around the English coast.

Hudson's kitchen lay off the entrance hall and was furnished with cherrywood settle and oak dresser, of the kind seen at Deanery

The entrance hall at Lindisfarne was made out of smaller rooms, their walls replaced by Romanesque pillars without bases or capitals. Visiting the castle in 1918, the effete writer Lytton Strachey felt he was immured in a stone tomb where 'any slip would mean instant death'.

Garden – so even the service side of the house shared in the general aesthetic. A stone tunnel leads down to the Ship Room, a sitting room with a model ship suspended from the ceiling, and the vaulted dining room, with brick floors laid with old Turkey rugs. At the top of the castle, shaped to form a Castle Drogo-like bastion, Lutyens created an Upper Gallery; it is lit with restraint, by small mullion windows. One end has a dais, reached by oak steps. It made a stage, faced by an audience who had their backs to the main windows, and would therefore not be distracted from the performance in front of them. This was the space consecrated to Suggia.

Augustus John painted an unforgettable image of Suggia – one of the few women whom James Bond thought looked elegant playing the cello – in a volcanic red dress, its folds so flowing that the canvas had to be enlarged to portray them; here is a fiery and creatively imperious individual. By contrast, an informal snap of her taken at Lindisfarne shows her with a foot playfully placed

Even the outwardly stuffy Edward Hudson could relax at Lindisfarne. Here he is seen imitating a dead tiger, while his grand amour, the Portuguese cellist Guilhermina Suggia places her foot on his shoulder. The castle was a wild, romantic caprice – inconvenient but Bohemian and fun.

BOOM IT LIKE ANYTHING

on top of Hudson, dressed in a blazer and cap. Hudson's crowd was arty. Not so the world of the Prince and Princess of Wales, future George V and Queen Mary, who rumbled over the sands in a procession of carriages in 1908 and failed to see the romance that so much inspired Lutyens and Huddy. It was an epic clash of cultural worlds. Lutyens, as ever, charmed the prince, but Hudson was 'dreadfully nervous' and the princess hurt her feet on the cobbles. The only thing they really admired was a fleur de lys on a fireback. Both Hudson and Lutyens had to lie down when they were gone.

Hudson's third country house was Plumpton Place, purchased in the late 1920s. A moated Saxon homestead had risen up the social scale to become a manor house, only to sink down again, after the Crimean War, when the owner, Lord Chichester, divided it into cottages. Lutyens was, characteristically, enthusiastic, immediately seeing the possibilities.

> My dear Huddy, lovely, lovely! Those millponds! You must have millions and millions of *roses*, d'you see? Reflected in the water – and water-falls – something like this.

Out came the pencil and paper to beguile his old friend. Hudson created a garden, with a shimmering cascade formed by overlapping paving tiles over which the water makes a pattern like a net. Two of the millponds had become marsh but were dug out again. But now in his seventies and feeling the economic cold of the Depression, Hudson never lived in the manor house, being content with a cottage called the Mill House for his own occupation. It had indeed been a mill, and Lutyens played up to the association by laying millstones in the paving – perhaps in ignorance of the fact that it had not been a cornmill, where millstones would have been needed to grind flour, but a fulling mill, which would have used hammers to beat cloth. The old manor house became something to look at rather than live in. Suggia would still play in the hall, when Huddy had guests, sitting at the end between bay windows to give light from either side: the effect that Lutyens had created on a more modest scale at Lindisfarne.

The landscape setting was all. 'Of course, I have arranged for two or three hundred roses,' he told 'My dear Miss Jekyll' in October 1928, his instincts having coincided with Lutyens's, '… just to get some sort of gardening effect next year'; his mind turned to the beauty of the 'tumbling roses' at Deanery Garden. In her mid eighties, Jekyll did not come to Plumpton herself but Hudson had photographs taken for her and asked Lutyens to send a full set of plans.

> What I want to do is to keep the planting quite simple through-out the place. I want it to look natural and as though it had always been there for hundreds of years. I don't want what I call the 'swagger' sort of gardening. I am very pleased with the Senecio of which the Duchess of Northumberland gave me quite a lot. These and water forget-me-nots, primroses, Solomon's seal, bluebells and ferns are the sort of things that I feel would look well.[4]

Thousands of spring bulbs were planted on the deep banks of the ponds. Hundreds of other plants came from the Munstead Wood nursery. In early 1929, Hudson wrote Jekyll 'a note of remembrance of all your kindness and the friendship you have given me and hon-oured me with for so many years', describing the 'gorgeous piece of luck' represented by the fall of a mighty elm tree during a storm; although he 'almost wept, it was such a superb tree,' this providen-tially opened views to the Downs and enabled a spring to rise. Cue the tapping of the spring and the creation of 'the most wonderful Primula Garden you can imagine'.

Hudson died in 1936 but *Country Life* continued to fight Lutyens's corner until his own death in 1944 and beyond. It commemorated him in the three mighty *Memorial Volumes* dedicated to his works and the Christopher Hussey biography. They continue to set a benchmark for architectural publishing; complete sets of the volumes now sell for thousands of pounds and they have been twice reprinted in facsimile. Not quite all of Lutyens's works were presented either in the *Memorial Volumes* or in the magazine. The image was curated. Houses that showed Art Nouveau tendencies or were too idiosyncratic were left out of the canon. Le Bois des Moutiers did not feature, nor Daneshill in Hampshire – whose walls are expanses of brick, relieved by square 'pugholes' (holes for scaffolding poles on medieval structures) decorated with different patterns of baked clay. (In 1901, Daneshill's client, the banker Walter Hoare, had been persuaded to open a brickworks specialising in the custom-made bricks that Lutyens had previously had to import from Holland; it supplied the bricks from which Daneshill was built two years later. The nearby brickworks office was, in itself, a pattern book of all the varieties of brick being produced.) In the twenty-first century, this sin of omission was expiated in part by the late Gavin Stamp, who sought out the non-canonical works and published a couple of them in *Country Life*.[5] This, however, is something of a footnote to the magazine's long-running campaign on behalf of its favourite architect. It was an unprecedented phenomenon. No previous architect in Britain had been championed in print to this extent – indeed no illustrated magazine, read by clients rather than the profession, had existed to do so.

Jobs came from Hudson's own circle – for example, the Dormy House which Lord Riddell commissioned to provide overnight accommodation for golfers using the Walton Heath Golf Club (Hudson joined him as one of the club's three owners). And the booming directly brought him three of his best clients. Lutyens met

77

Mrs Belville, whose husband Frank, the maker of Robinson's Barley Water, commissioned the 'butterfly-plan' house Papillon Hall at a weekend party at Deanery Garden. Julius Drewe wrote to Hudson, as proprietor of *Country Life*, about whom he should ask to design Castle Drogo: unsurprisingly Lutyens was put forward as 'the only possible choice'. Hudson also recommended him to the Portmans, who created a beautiful garden to go with their ugly Victorian house at Hestercombe – it was a chance for Lutyens to realise the garden of the white house of the casket he had made for Emily before they were married. Herbert Johnson saw Crooksbury, Lutyens's very first house, in *Country Life*; and the result was Marsh Court.

Hestercombe was one of over a hundred gardens that Lutyens created with Gertrude Jekyll. Here, the structure is provided by classical features such as piers, arches and balustrades, given a rustic quality by the rough stone out of which they are made.

FOUR

TIGER, TIGER

Marsh Court, Hampshire 1901–4

Prowling tiger: a typically witty Lutyens doodle that incorporates the insignia and initials on the letterpaper of the P&O shipping line on which he crossed to India in 1912.

L UTYENS'S CLIENTS BEFORE THE FIRST WORLD War were an index of Edwardian society – not 'Society' so much as the economically dynamic individuals who were making money. Few came from old aristocratic families, although many apparently new fortunes were supplemented with inherited wealth, usually quite recently made. Sir George Sitwell was unusual: a Conservative (albeit not so double-dyed as to stop him from campaigning for his son Osbert when he stood for the Liberal party) from an old family, whose house Renishaw was black with dust from his coal mines. Only Willie James and his petite, short-sighted wife, wrapped in furs, belonged to the Marlborough House Set which surrounded the Prince of Wales, future Edward VII; Mrs James was said to be either his wife or – according to her son, the Surrealist Edward James – his daughter. (Willie James, a big game hunter until his brother Frank was killed by a wounded elephant, had inherited part of an American mining fortune.) John Horner's family had been at Mells since the Dissolution of the Monasteries and his wife, the beautiful Frances Horner, a great friend of Lutyens, was one of The Souls: she inherited money and paintings from her father who was a Graham of Graham's port. But they were not rich by the standards of the plutocracy. Nor was Princess Louise for whom Lutyens remodelled the Ferry Inn at Rosneath, west of Glasgow. She never used it.

More typical of Lutyens's clients was the large clutch of bankers, such as Walter Hoare at Daneshill, Cecil Baring at Lambay and Mark Fenwick at Abbotswood (his wife Molly Clayton was a member of a Northumbrian banking family). Cyril Flower, Lord Battersea, parading along the Norfolk beach where Lutyens was building The Pleasaunce, in white silk with a towel or a camera around his neck, was a banker of sorts, but additionally married a Rothschild; a homosexual scandal would later become an embarrassment. Nearby, Lord Hillingdon, a partner in Glyn Mills bank, built Overstrand Hall. The law was represented by Alfred Lyttelton, a Liberal MP and keen sportsman, who commissioned Greywalls – originally High Walls – at Gullane, so he could play golf; the barrister William Chance, who had first seen Gertrude Jekyll up a ladder at Munstead, commissioned Orchards with the proceeds from a family glass-making business; and the Farrer brothers of Lincoln's Inn built The Salutation, Sandwich. Sir Edgar Horne at Tigbourne Court was chairman of the Prudential Insurance Company. Life assurance was a relatively new and progressive industry, which offered security in old age to those who had made provision for it.

Princess Dolgorouki at Nashdom had begun her life as plain Fanny Wilson, heiress to a shipping fortune. She married a Russian prince in middle age. Nashdom means Our Home in Russian; Lutyens could not help designing in the style of John Nash. Frederick Mirrielees, the client at Goddards, had married the heiress of the Cunard Line, whose ocean liners glamorously plied the Atlantic: he had previously been concerned in a family department store in Russia. At Ashby St Ledgers, Lord Wimborne was a major industrialist who owned steel mills. Few clients were rich on that scale, unless one counts Lady Phillips, the wife of the South African 'Randlord' Sir Lionel Phillips: Lutyens designed an art gallery for her in Johannesburg — although, when he was temporarily banished from South Africa for his part in the Jameson

Raid, it was not Lutyens that Sir Lionel asked to build Tylney Hall but Weir Schultz. Lutyens's first client, Arthur 'Chippy' Chapman of Crooksbury had also done well overseas; he made enough money from a jute business in India to retire early (and to cause Lutyens some unnecessary jealousy when he went around with Lady Emily). Colonel Spencer, for whom Lutyens built Lascombe, was another figure of the Empire: he had commanded the Camel Corps during the Berber Campaign, although his money must have come from elsewhere. (His recommendation of a Camel Corps soldier to be Lutyens's shorthand secretary proved disastrous: the man absconded with £400.) Nathaniel Lloyd's money came from colour printing; he built Great Dixter and became an authority on brickwork. Mrs Streatfield, the motorist at Fulbrook, was a brewer's daughter. Ernest Blackburn of Little Thakeham had been a schoolmaster until he inherited money. Julius Drewe of Castle Drogo owned a chain of grocery stores. Hugh Lane, for whom Lutyens remodelled Lindsey House on Cheyne Walk, had worked his way up from his beginnings as an assistant at Colnaghi to a commanding position in the art market. It was Lane who introduced him to Arthur Grenfell, a City speculator who commissioned Lutyens to enlarge Roehampton House on the way out of London going south-west. Speculation was disreputable. The boom-and-bust pursuit of stockbroking was not much better: a get-rich-quick scheme for the traders and their friends, such as Lloyd George and his political colleagues who used inside knowledge to benefit from the rise in Marconi's Wireless Telegraph Company shares in 1912 – the coup came back to bite them in the form of the Marconi Scandal. Herbert Johnson of Marsh Court was a stockbroker. He was not only a buccaneer but a fisherman: Lutyens loved him.

Born in 1856, Johnson was the son of a clergyman schoolmaster, the Rev. Henry Johnson, whose health failed after he took on his father's debts.[1] A way out of his difficulties seemed to come from

Port Elizabeth in the Cape, where he was appointed to run two schools. Inadequate accommodation, expensive food, mosquitos, a succession of assistant masters who soon left for the diamond fields – although the family battled gamely against adversity for nine years, Mrs Johnson, who was carrying her tenth child, had to go home. The others followed, Johnnie (as Lutyens called him) at the age of sixteen. He was good at mathematics. Beginning his career as an office boy to a stock jobber, he showed his worth by compiling Johnson's Tables, a new way of calculating interest. By the time he commissioned Marsh Court in 1901, he had made half a million, and if the wind sometimes went out of his sails, he could, at the age of forty-five, get it back again. At that point unmarried, he did not care what he spent on his house.

Johnnie had come to the Test some years before, when he bought Marsh Court Farm, with two miles of riverbank, fish-rearing ponds, eel weirs, partridge and duck shooting, farm buildings and two hundred and seventy-nine acres. Every weekend during the fishing season he would take the train from Waterloo to Andover Junction, changing onto the Sprat and Winkle Line to Stockbridge, a mile and a half from Marsh Court. Over the winter, he would come down to shoot wildfowl. Of course he read the newly founded *Country Life*. In September 1900 Hudson published his first piece on a house by Lutyens: Crooksbury near Farnham, his earliest commission. Johnnie saw a good thing and bought Lutyens shares on a rising market.

Next March, Johnnie invited Ned to the Test, where they fished, ate a late lunch and discussed building plans. Everything would be left to Lutyens. 'Tiger, tiger!' he wrote to Emily, starting the drawings at once. 'I do love Johnson,' he later wrote. They fished, studied Lutyens's drawings until midnight and, next morning, galloped over the Downs, with Lutyens mounted on a seventeen-hand hunter, despite not having ridden since the time of his marriage in 1897.

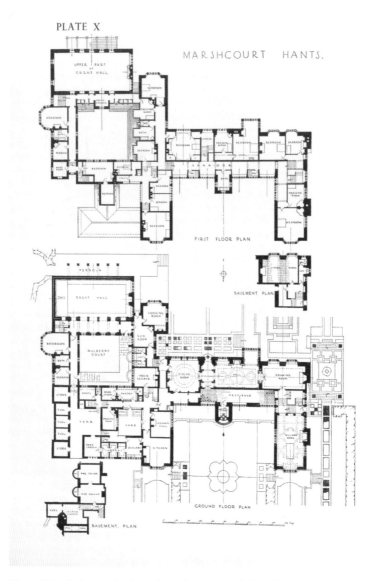

PLATE X

MARSHCOURT HANTS.

FIRST FLOOR PLAN

BASEMENT PLAN

GROUND FLOOR PLAN

BASEMENT PLAN

Plan of Marsh Court. The front door does not lead directly to the hall, which is entered at one end by a kind of screens passage. A wall opposite the door into the drawing room blocks the view of the garden, which is then seen through windows to either side.

Over the four years that the house took to build, client and architect became friends. In a fog of smoke from Lutyens's pipe and Johnson's cigars, conversation continued long into the night, with alcoholic stimulants to hand. 'And the more we drink together,' concludes a ditty in one of Lutyens's sketchbooks, 'the merrier we shall be.'

On a shoulder of previously bare hill, overlooking the River Test in Hampshire, this quite dazzling house was built of clunch, a kind of hardened chalk or soft limestone which is easily cut when it is first quarried. Though soft, it has been used quite widely in counties without better building materials, principally for humble structures such as cottages and boundary walls. For durability, it was usually plastered over, as a protection from the elements. Occasionally it can be seen in church towers and castle walls, or as part of a chequer-board with brick or flint, and on the Berkshire Downs, the elegant façades of Ashdown House are built of it. Clearly, however, it was less than wholly practical – and could be avoided completely in an age of railway transport. And yet at Marsh Court clunch was used *con amore*, in broad masses, interrupted by a scattering of small squares of red tile or knapped flint. From a distance, the effect is that of a shimmering palace.

To keep its pristine colour and to prevent weathering, the walls of Marsh Court have to be regularly limewashed, allowing approximately one coat for each year the application is expected to last. Each block has to be individually painted to avoid washing over the mortar joints, which would spoil the look. Make the mistake of leaning against one of the walls and your shoulder will turn white with limewash and chalk. But hang the inconvenience and expense! Lutyens was little over thirty when he designed Marsh Court, and both he and Johnnie delighted in the bravura effect of this *jeu d'esprit*.

Marsh Court was Lutyens's most thoroughgoing expression of the Arts and Crafts diktat that buildings should be created as far as possible from materials found on site. In 1898, Ernest Gimson had designed Stoneywell Cottage in Leicestershire, now owned by the National Trust, as practically an emanation of the rocky outcrop on which it is perched. A couple of years after Marsh Court, whose design dates from 1901, E.S. Prior built Voewood, on the North Norfolk coast, out of a seemingly mad combination of pebbles, brick, tile and flint – everything except the glass being found locally. Chalk, as any fisherman knows, gives the Test valley its character. It provides a habitat special to southern England, home to eighty per cent of all the chalk streams in the world. Of chalk Marsh Court would be built. Lutyens, being Lutyens, took this theme to an extreme. Not only are the exterior walls faced in clunch, but quite a lot of the interior also features it, including the epic billiard table – players could chalk their cues on the base. For the outside of the house, the blocks — quarried nearby, slung onto ash poles and carried to the site by horses – were dressed as ashlar, elevating it from the condition of rubble as which it has often been used in building. And yet the ashlar blocks are not perfect. Protruding flints, found in beds of chalk, were not cut out, nor the blocks containing them rejected; Lutyens insisted that they were kept to emphasise the organic quality of the material.

But Marsh Court was, nevertheless, Arts and Crafts with a twist. Lutyens had always wanted to build a white house, for reasons that had nothing to do with Ruskin and Morris. He was a romantic. He and Emily had been meant to inhabit a white house, as we saw from the green leather casket. That white house was never realised. Despite its much bigger scale, Marsh Court is still imbued with a similar idealism. Sadly, the spring-like optimism with which Marsh Court was conceived could not be sustained into old age, when the buccaneer was becalmed. Eventually Johnson had to sell the house. But never did he criticise Lutyens for impracticality. Like Julius Drewe at Castle Drogo, who knew at an early stage that his castle could not keep out the water but seems never to have thought of suing the architect, he must have felt it had been a *folie à deux*. To quote Johnson's obituary in *The Times* (April 13, 1949): it became 'for the rest of his life the very symbol of himself', and he loved every stone of it.

By the 1920s, Marsh Court had an estate of over one thousand two hundred acres. As Master of the Hursley Hunt, his greatest day came when he killed a fox, fished a trout and shot a brace of partridge, all on his own land. But this was not a big landscape. Overlooking the Test, with its water meadows and silvery willows, the house was designed to be long and low, so that its size did not overwhelm this delicate, very English scene. Typically, it was approached by a Picturesque route: the drive leads off a wooded lane, before burrowing through a cutting made in a hillside; it then goes past the house, although you cannot yet see it, before swinging around in a broad arc to bring the visitor to an elm-boarded 'power house' that serves, visually, as a lodge. The power house was joined, in 1927, by a garage, barn-like in form but beautifully built, with round columns made of thin bricks in the courtyard. Together these form the kind of entrance that Lutyens liked: a grand house – Berrydown, Great Maytham, The Salutation, Plumpton Place – is approached through a screen of vernacular buildings. From here, the last lap of the drive to Marsh Court runs straight over a small bridge to the north-facing entrance court – straight but not entirely predictably, for Lutyens does not align it on the front door.

Summer garden-party guests walked directly to the Jekyll-planted gardens. These include a sunken water garden, where fountains of seahorses and tortoises, made by Lady (Julia) Chance, wife of Lutyens's client at Orchards, directed water jets into a tank planted with water lilies. The space pretends to occupy the shell of a room demolished at some previous period. Mixed materials at the base of the walls of the house itself also imply a history that never was; they suggest that Marsh Court stands on the footings of an earlier building. Here the little squares that appear randomly across the great expanses of clunch derive from the pugholes left for scaffolding to be fitted that appear on medieval walls. Lutyens loved the Mannerist contrast between broad swathes of wall and almost miniaturist decoration, seen also, a couple of years later, at Daneshill House in Berkshire.

We enter through the door, sunk into a porch, on the north front. The porch is one of Lutyens's most brilliant inventions, displaying his complete mastery of materials in a blaze of geometrical bravado. A semicircular arch mirrors the shape of the barrel vault above it, the latter patterned with syncopated squares of tile and clunch. The squares reappear in the floor. Despite the largeness of the conception, the actual size – as often with Lutyens – is almost teasingly small. This heightens the apparent opposites of cosiness and drama.

The door opens into a long, broad lateral passage or vestibule. Once again, Lutyens is sending the visitor on an oblique or round-about route to the main rooms, heightening the sense of discovery and anticipation.

The anticipation here is, perhaps, misplaced. The enfilade of rooms along the garden front is, as near as such a thing is possible in a house by Lutyens, dull. Still, there are quirks. The hall is entered at one end, as though there had once been a medieval screens passage, subsequently replaced by clusters of Tuscan columns. The room is a herald of the 'Wrennaissance' manner that would develop fully around 1905. For now it is an example of Lutyens's genius for jumbling an eclectic mix of architectural styles to make new forms. He did something similar at Little Thakeham, where the screens passage of the hall is expressed in the language of Hawksmoor. The stone of the outside of the house invades this indoor space – hardly warm, hardly comfortable, but oh so dramatic. The garland of fruit,

Marsh Court: a glittering fairy palace whose clunch walls shine white above the River Test in Hampshire. The style is Elizabethan, although the walled garden – shown here – is a piece of instant history, evoking the foundations of an earlier house.

The drama of the entrance porch. The otherwise freestanding arch over the opening is tied to a vault of irregular chequerwork by enormous keystones. Herbert Johnson, a buccaneering stockbroker, was one of Lutyens's favourite clients.

flowers and ribbons that decorates the hall ceiling, conceivably inspired by the *Country Life* article on Groombridge Place, Kent, which appeared in 1903, is not made from plaster but carved from chalk. To one side of the hall lies the dining room, entirely panelled in quartered walnut, whose sleekness is practically Art Deco. On the other side, the drawing room overlooks the water garden – though Lutyens intrigues visitors by not showing it on axis; it can only be glimpsed off centre from the two windows.

Equipped with a large house, Johnson had, apparently, no thoughts of a wife until 1912, when he met Violet Meeking, the widow of an officer who died from enteric fever during the Boer War. He was fifty-six and a rich man. She was forty, with two daughters, several hunters and an insufficient income. Changes were made at Marsh Court. In his bachelor days, Johnson had been accompanied on fishing trips by his chauffeur, John Cliff, who would sing music-hall songs to the banjo. On Cliff's marriage to a housemaid, Lutyens was commissioned to provide suitable accommodation. The new Mrs Johnson, however, brought her own chauffeur. Tension was only defused when Cliff volunteered for the Royal Flying Corps in 1914.

Paradoxically, the war cemented the Johnsons' marriage, giving them, as well as Mrs Johnsons's two daughters, a common cause in the hospitals that they founded in Stockbridge and on the Marsh Court estate. The ladies worked in them tirelessly, while Johnson paid. Alas, in 1921 Mrs Johnson died. Johnson resumed a life of sport. Big-game hunting in Africa was combined with yachting and the mastership of the Hursley Hunt. It was to accommodate the Hunt Ball that Lutyens built his last work at Marsh Court, the ballroom or Play Hall, as he called it. Storm clouds would gather during the Recession and Johnnie – widowed and blind – had to leave his beloved home; but for now the sun shone, almost as it had during Marsh Court's Edwardian zenith.

FIVE

WHAT FUN IT WOULD BE

Lambay Castle, Ireland 1905–12
Tomb of Maude Baring 1922
Chapel at Lambay 1925
The White House, Lambay 1932

A self-doodle from one of the Lambay guest books. 'Father', wrote Lutyens's daughter Mary, 'always seemed at his happiest with the Barings.'

I F MARSH COURT STANDS FOR FAIRYTALE ROMANCE, Lambay represents another aspect of Lutyens's genius at its most profound – poetry. This country house on an island near Dublin, three miles from the mainland of Ireland, transcends the usual meaning of architecture, as a series of built forms concentrated in an obvious structure. The main buildings are the centrepiece of a landscape that has been controlled to create a piece of theatre as you walk through it. This not theatre of a purely dramatic kind but theatre as the Greeks understood it, as part of their sacred rites. At Lambay, this is conveyed through building materials that have largely been dug from the site itself, in Arts and Crafts manner, and are used with a sensitivity that deserves to be called sacramental; despite the remote location and informal character of the life that the house served, the size of each stone in an arch or decorative feature was carefully considered and must have been meticulously drawn in the office before being erected.

Furthermore, those arches and features often incorporate parts of a circle – indeed, the whole of Lutyens's work at Lambay as a meditation on the circle, whose shape appears not merely in the great enclosing wall that he built to define the sanctum of the habitation and separate it from the hill and farmland beyond, but in a host of less formal contexts: a round of lawn edged by stones, a path mown in meadowgrass, the curving apron of pebbles laid in front of a farm gate which describes not just one semicircle, but two

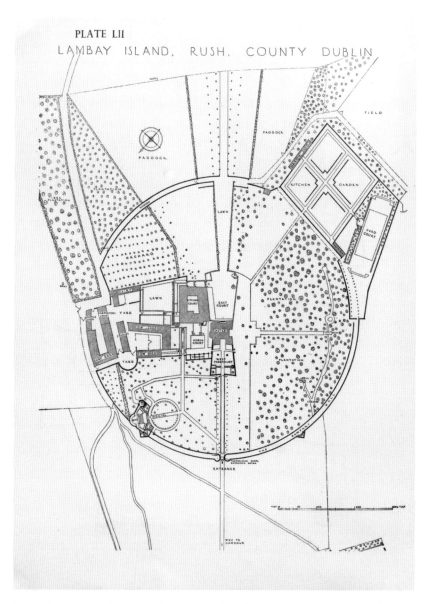

PLATE LII

LAMBAY ISLAND, RUSH, COUNTY DUBLIN

Plan of Lambay Island. On entering the walled enclosure, you approach the castle along a narrow avenue of trees, aligned to the old building. Lutyens's new wing is only revealed as you reach the forecourt.

semicircles with different centres. Lambay is both the apogee of the style imbued in Lutyens by Gertrude Jekyll and the first sustained revelation of the intense feeling for geometry (an expression, for a poor attender at church, of the divine) which characterises the second half of his career. The sense of mystery continues inside the house, where the play of the light, as it penetrates the thick walls, is as important to Lutyens's effect as the shapes conjured from stone or wood.

Lutyens was always at his best when working for friends. Cecil and Maude Baring, for whom he created Lambay, were among his favourite clients. The Hon. Cecil Baring could not have been more different from Herbert Johnson. Cecil's father, the 1st Baron Revelstoke and head of Barings Bank, was remembered by Cecil's brother Maurice as collecting Bréguet watches so he could give them away to people he liked, and Cecil grew up in the luxury of Mayfair and Membland Hall, in Devon. Although he enjoyed shooting animals as much as other rich Etonians and kept a stee-plechaser while at Oxford, his cast of mind was intellectual. He

After arriving at the little dock, all you see of Lambay Castle is this wall with trees rising above it. There is an irresistible air of mystery and folklore.

94

was a brilliant Classicist, who took a first in Greats and supposedly kept a copy of Sophocles or Aeschylus in the drawer of his desk at Barings; one of Maude's nicknames for him was Caesar – albeit from his early loss of hair rather than his Latin learning. In the wake of Darwin and Huxley's theories, he took a keen interest in the natural sciences, in pursuit of which he would be oblivious to all else. As his daughter Daphne Pollen recalled,

> At Lambay he wore whitish tweeds, knickerbockers and a close-fitting tweed cap. His way, for instance, of walking unhesitatingly into a rock pool to examine its contents, without pausing to remove his well-burnished brogues, still less to change them afterwards, was to us a source of great vicarious pleasure and admiration, as was the knowledge that when he made expeditions to the back of the island before dawn to watch the grey seals, he would wade waist deep across to the small island which was their basking ground and lie there in his wet clothes, concealed with his camera, waiting for the light.[1]

He would handle lizards and young owls without regard for their possible stings and bites. Today the rhea and Japanese cranes that delighted Lutyens may have gone but wallabies still bound vigorously around the hills (although they were not introduced until the 1950s). Baring loved music and had a beautiful singing voice.

Maude also had a gilded childhood. Her father Pierre Lorillard IV was part of a tobacco dynasty, who came to own – once he had bought his siblings out of their part in the inheritance, a reputed six hundred thousand acres of upstate New York, once territory of the Algonquin peoples; there he founded Tuxedo Park, a residential community of lawns, tennis courts and boat house, based around a clubhouse and entered via imposing gates. His energy and success at Tuxedo were matched by his prowess as a racehorse owner. The youngest of four siblings by ten years, Maude grew up to be a prime example of the phenomenon that was cutting swathes through the younger male ranks of European society: the 'American girl' (which is to say, the American girl who was also an heiress). At a time when conventional wisdom, in aristocratic houses, held that female offspring needed little education because their future in life would be assured through marriage (and men might be put off by signs of cleverness), young American women were miracles of accomplishment, lively and able to converse on a wide range of subjects. In *Daisy Miller*, Henry James describes the dilemma of Count Otto who

> could immediately think of a dozen men he knew who had married American girls. There appeared now to be a constant danger of marrying the American girl: it was something one had to reckon with, like the railway, the telegraph, the discovery of dynamite, the Chassepot rifle, the Socialistic spirit: it was one of the complications of modern life.

With her eighteen-inch waist and glossy black hair, Maude could ride, drive a carriage, fence and play golf; friends would watch her play tennis simply for the elegance with which she did it. 'She is very American, very dark,' wrote a bemused Lutyens in 1906. Her feistiness had not deserted her:

> She gave a funny account of herself just before Calypso [her second daughter] came and she was big with her, deer stalking with Baring and how she could only get down the hills by roll-ing, she was so fat and round. I can't imagine everybody doing this, can you? Fancy her strength.

Baring may have been Maude's superior in education but it is easy to see why he fell for her. For her part, Baring was unlike anyone she had ever met and she reciprocated his love.

Cecil had gone to New York some years before the Baring Crisis of 1890, when risky Argentinian investments turned bad and Barings was nearly brought down, and stayed there until 1902, working for a partnership formed between Barings and an American bank. There, a project for his leisure time was the building of a tennis court at Tuxedo with a friend and client of the bank, Thomas Suffern Tailer. Maude was Tailer's wife. The couple had a four-year-old son called Lorillard or 'Larry', but it was an unhappy marriage. Risking scandal and, as it would turn out, losing the opportunity to watch over or even see Larry as he grew up, Maude divorced her husband. She and Cecil were married in a London registry office in 1902.

The Barings' story illustrates the tempests that shook the Edwardian age, apt to be regarded, with hindsight, as a golden afternoon before the onset of the First World War but which was as tumultuous, for those who lived through it, as any other. This can be seen at all levels of national life. Music-hall enthusiasm for the Empire could not hide the weakness of Britain's industry, which was being outpaced by Germany and the United States. The Boer War had been a shameful near-disaster. Revolution was brewing in Ireland. Lloyd George's People's Budget of 1909, intended to 'wage implacable warfare against poverty and squalidness', was so truculently opposed by Conservative peers that the House of Lords was reformed two years later. In a message to the future that Canon Samuel Barnett wrote on the completion of the spire of Lutyens's St Jude's church in Hampstead Garden Suburb in 1913, he described the period of unrest in which the church had been constructed.

In China and in India great changes have occurred; in Eastern Europe the peoples of the Balkans have driven out the Turks; in

97

the older Nations the fear of War has dominated politics: and here in England the movements of workmen and of women are threatening the accustomed order of Society.

Cecil and Maude's drama was more personal: a rebellion against the rules that underpinned 'the accustomed order of Society', which Barnett praised. Their marriage was a source of complexity and even darkness – Maude's isolation from Larry – as well as joy. Was Lambay bought as a place remote from the world in which they would normally have moved, where the guilty couple could hide themselves away? The answer is no. Divorce was difficult but not unknown in 1902. On his return from the US, Cecil stepped back from the bank but returned to it in 1909, becoming a director and managing director in 1911 – roles that he kept until the end of his life. In London, they bought a conspicuous house in Portland Place (demolished in the 1920s to make way for Broadcasting House). They had lived in the equally prominent Avenue Rapp in Paris; it was from there that they began the negotiations to buy Lambay.

Both Maude and Cecil came from families who were habitual builders of houses: the work at Lambay fits that pattern. It was undoubtedly a retreat, with much of the Spartan simplicity of Lindsifarne – but only in the sense of being a private realm where the couple and their children could live an ideal life. This included, once Cecil had taught Maude the language, reading Greek literature together and the study of wildlife. On Cecil's death, Maurice wrote that those who came into contact with his mind 'were conscious of having adventured into a country of serenity and light: of breathing a gracious air and entering a quiet citadel'. It could be a description of Lambay.

The Barings were in Bavaria, for Wagner operas, when Cecil saw an advertisement for the island in *The Field*. It would be the start of an adventure. Sailing over with the postman, he saw a volcanic outcrop rising to four hundred feet. The boat put in at a tiny harbour, near a row of white-walled coastguard cottages, still occupied by some grumpy coastguards. He must then have walked over the fields to the old stronghold, made up of four harled towers with splayed walls and crow-stepped gables. Beyond some barns, a walled kitchen garden and a chapel, that was the extent of the architecture. He bought it. Realising that the house was barely habitable, he employed a Dublin architect – his name now forgotten – to upgrade it, without great architectural fanfare. But the work proved unsatisfactory and water poured in. It is believed that Baring learnt of Lutyens from reading *Country Life*, although it is difficult to think that he had not already met some of his clients. He could not as yet have read the architectural description of 'Lindisfarne Castle, Northumberland: a Residence of Mr Edward Hudson' because that did not appear until 1913, but had he heard tell of the castle? If so, the case might have seemed very similar to his own.

With children the same age, the Lutyens and Baring families would often spend Christmas together, with Ned remembered as 'the best and gayest of hosts – no one, however young or timid, would be left out of the general jollity'.[2] It was Cecil who paid for the black and white marble floor at Mansfield Street, after Lutyens bought the house in 1919; he would also help his friend over what Lutyens, with his soft 'r', described as 'money wowwies'. Together they plotted a marriage between Cecil's daughter Calypso and Ned's son Robert, a surely disastrous union, had it happened, the only redeeming feature of which would have been the house that Lutyens intended to design for them on Cheyne Walk. There was already a family connection, however, since Lutyens was godfather to the Barings' son Rupert. To Lutyens, the warmth of the Baring family amid the wilds of Lambay made a painful contrast to his own fractured home life in London.

The Barings very kind, very amusing is the life, the children affectionate and nice to me. The house all pulled to pieces and they live in three cottages up the hill and I slept in a room near the harbour so I had a long walk for my meals. How you would love Lambay… I do envy them their life and oh what fun it would be with you and you would love the air and freedom of it all – all four square, sea side, mountain to yourself and family.[3]

To Jane Brown, Lutyens's 'best-beloved clients' often had 'as their defining characteristic, an innate, perhaps subconscious need for order'.[4] As a result, they were naturally attracted to each other, forming webs of friendship or connections through marriage.

The fun that Lutyens and his clients had at Lambay is reflected in the amount of time that Ned worked there. Although the rainwater hoppers and date stones declare 1910 to have been the end of the project, that only concluded phase one. Additions and alterations continued for another twenty-five years.

Lambay shows Lutyens at his most subtle. Today, the approach to the dock presents a few more buildings than Baring found on his first trip. The coastguard cottages (the coastguards themselves having been soon expelled) are still there, joined by a White House, around a courtyard, built for the grandchildren and nannies in 1933 (Lutyens called it Babylon – a place for babies); nearby is a court for Cecil's sporting passion, real tennis, looking like a military blockhouse. Your bags are unloaded from the boat; you see across a trackless field a great circular enclosure, with nothing showing of what lies inside beyond the sycamore trees and Scots pine. As John Goodall recently described in *Country Life*, 'Like something out of an Irish fairytale, the boughs of the trees have been shaped into a great dome by the wind.'[5] The 'Chinese wall', as Lutyens called it, is not quite circular, since two triangular fleches project from each side, so that defenders could enfilade anyone attacking the gate.

Standing between bastions, the gate is a memory of the Surrey Style, with oak braces and, along the top, a detail derived from the staircase at Munstead Wood; but is there also a suggestion of the temple gateways seen in Japanese prints? The openwork does not pretend to be remotely defensible but gives access to a sacred space: the sanctuary of Home.

There is an avenue, then another enclosure containing a garden, planted (though she never went there) by Gertrude Jekyll. This is the west court, balanced on the further side of the house by the east court: both wedge-shaped, their canted sides suggesting that they are segments of circles. Further progress involves crossing – perhaps with symbolic intent – a rill, ending at one end in a circular pool. Close to, you can see that the walls of the castle, built in the sixteenth century, are harled with little pebbles of 'Lambay porphyry',

Penetrating the gateway in the outer wall, you are enticed down an avenue towards the old castle, seen here. Lutyens restored it, à la Lindisfarne, created a terraced garden and added a service wing, sunken to reduce visual impact.

a dark greenish stone in a creamy grey mortar, mottled with tan-coloured lichen. Windows and doors are faced with limestone from Skerries, a near point on the mainland, over which are narrow Classical dripstones to keep off the water. Then, as you seek to enter the house, comes a typical Lutyens ambiguity: two identical silvery oak doors, one on the side return of each tower. They are opened by ironwork handles designed as linked hearts.

Inside, the principal rooms – as at Lindisfarne – seem to be hewn from the rock, although most of them were pre-existing and shelter beneath old and lumpy vaults. Joining two of the old rooms together to form the sitting room gave Lutyens the chance to create a degree of spatial complexity, by setting the connecting arch at an angle; to

Granite overmantel in the main bedroom. The joints between the stones are exactly aligned on the centres of the three segments in the geometrical motif but elsewhere small variations break the symmetry to provide animation.

WHAT FUN IT WOULD BE

the north it breaks out into a bay, expressed externally as a gaunt tower, presaging the style of Castle Drogo. Old photographs show a model galleon hanging from the arch, as at Lindisfarne. There are two staircases. The lowest flights of the Wood Stair are actually of black stone, set between walls that narrow in false perspective. The Stone Stair is a spiral, based on two circles. Circles and segments of circles appear throughout the house, particularly in fireplaces, as well as garden steps. Family memory has it that Lutyens saw segments of circles as expressive of welcome – an encouragement to move onto the next experience. Walls are whitewashed but the floorboards may be painted crimson or – in the White House for children and nannies – royal blue.

The result of all this was, by Edwardian standards, a house of small and strangely shaped rooms: indeed, in 1909 Lutyens describes the family as living happily in three cottages. While the Barings preferred simplicity over grandeur and Maude 'hated going to a big house too full of servants' such as Flete, the great Victorian house built by Lord Mildmay, a partner in Barings,[6] the accommodation at Lambay fell short of any Edwardian conception of a well-ordered existence: for this, kitchen, pantry, store rooms and servants' hall were required. So Lutyens added a courtyard at the south-west corner of the house, sinking it into the earth so that the pantiled roofs come almost to the ground. These walls are made from what looks like a nougat of boulders, dug from the site. Here was an opportunity to create a terraced garden, which provided the harvest of stone used to build the circular Great Wall of China. Beyond the courtyard comes a farm steading, one of whose barns adjoins the circular wall.

There is a suggestion that the charm may have rubbed off temporarily, a couple of years after the house was (for the time being) completed, for in August 1913 Lutyens wrote: 'They are back in love with the place again.'[7] Did they think it was just too impractical and inconvenient? The Barings restored a sailing boat called the *Shamrock* in 1904 and it remained the only means of reaching the island until 1922. When the *Shamrock* was becalmed, it could take three hours to make the crossing, with rowing. To do it in less than an hour was a cause for celebration. New projects arose, such as the restoration of the nineteenth-century chapel, to which Lutyens added a rugged Doric portico made of granite, with thin bands of slate beneath the capital. When Maude Baring died, still in her forties, in 1922, it was on Lambay she was buried, in a mausoleum tucked into one of the fleches of the Great Wall, in the monumental manner of Lutyens's war cemeteries in France.

Lambay was accompanied by other commissions from Cecil Baring. From 1924 he had been toying with the idea of building an art gallery on Cheyne Walk, next to what had been Maude's private studio, to house his collection of porcelain; this he abandoned in favour of a house for Calypso and her husband Guy Liddell. It lasted less than five years, being demolished in 1935 to make way for a block of flats; by then Cecil Baring, who had inherited his brother's title of Lord Revelstoke, was dead. Lambay has fared better. It is now that rarest of all things – a Lutyens house, loved, little changed and complete with its original contents. Nothing has been taken off the island. It is cherished by its family as Cecil and Maude Baring would have hoped, as the haven where their descendants can meet in the place of special harmony that Lutyens made for them.

SIX

THE HIGH GAME

Country Life Offices 1904

Heathcote, Yorkshire 1905–7

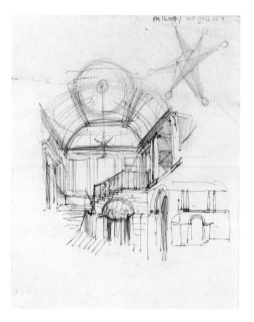

Sketch for the hall at Heathcote, the highly architectural villa which Lutyens built for J.T. Hemingway at Ilkley, Yorkshire, in 1906. Floor and stair were marble. The star-shaped light fitting would have been a bold response to the problem of the electric light bulb.

I T WAS 1906 AND JOHN THOMAS HEMINGWAY DIDN'T
stand a chance. A Yorkshireman, he had started work for the
wool exporters George Richardson & Company in Bradford;
by the time he was forty, he had made sufficient money to take
his family away from Bradford's Canal Road to the Victorian spa
town of Ilkley and commute from there. They lived in a house
with a big garden, called The Grove. There, they pursued a quiet
existence, spent far less than John earnt, and seem not to have
been noticed by the committees that ran the usual social round
of a prosperous community – which may have been somewhat
pleased with itself; perhaps the Hemingways were too newly
arrived to be allowed in, prosperous enough but looked down
upon. If John was the prominent Conservative and freemason
that the *Manchester Guardian* described on his death in 1926,
his activities did not attract newspaper interest during his life.
Evidently, he continued to work, since he was by then a hosiery
manufacturer with investments; but the *Guardian*'s short obituary
reads strangely, concentrating on a statement in his will about
charitable gifts to the effect that he had made sufficient during
his lifetime for more not to be needed. They had nothing to say
about other achievements, let alone his remarkable house.[1] And
yet he had given his children expensive educations in France
and Germany and would make a bold aesthetic choice by asking
Lutyens to design a home that would be a notch up from The

Grove: a place of status and comfort to reward a lifetime of toil. Lutyens ate him for breakfast.

Having grown up in the intimate green landscape of Surrey, Lutyens recoiled from the rawness of Yorkshire, some of whose stone naturally goes black with time – although you would have hardly known it, as every surface was black from the smoking chimneys of mill towns like Bradford. He also reacted badly to Ilkley, 'an ultra-suburban locality' as he called it. The villas were odious to him. In this he would have been supported by Ruskin, William Morris and Bumps; it was in reaction to the spread of such architecture, made from industrially produced materials, that the Arts and Crafts Movement had been created. In Lutyens's case there was more than a hint of snobbery about it. As he wrote to Emily, whom Hemingway had inadvertently called Mrs Lutyens:

> You would have fits … a coursed breakfast in slippers, boots put on in the sitting room sometimes used as a dining room and furnished as such – en suite but not so expensive as the real dining room. The ornaments – oh lor! and the walls of lincrusta with painted dado and frieze of flying sparrows, ferns and polyantha displayed. And then a mass of modern prints from Academy pictures and electric light galore. The doors very shiny and painted in a curious way – brown chocolate, blue and gold.

Lutyens mocked the family with its aspirations and appetite for motoring. But when going through the plans for Heathcote, the house that he would build for them, he discovered that Hemingway was far richer than he had thought. He had an income of £20,000 a year, which would increase once he had bought out his partner, but spent only £3,000 a year. For their means, the family lived modestly, despite the motors. Lutyens would educate them on how to spend money on building. He designed a house that was far beyond their needs and must have been the talk of Ilkley, if not Bradford and Leeds. In *Lutyens and the Edwardians*, Jane Brown believes that Lutyens was motivated by competition with Herbert Baker whom he had just seen in South Africa, a virgin land for architecture which Baker was populating with houses (of which he built a couple of hundred), churches, railway stations, civic buildings and monuments. Ilkley was not so virgin, but he would nevertheless use the opportunity that Hemingway gave him to show what he could do, and give villadom one in the eye.

Heathcote was a prime example of what Lutyens described as the High Game, one of his earliest sustained essays in Classicism. Lutyens's discovery of the style has been hailed as a Damascene conversion, which set his architecture – and architecture generally – on a new course. Like other aspects of the Lutyens myth, this is only partly true. For one thing, neither Classicism nor the geometry that underpins it were wholly new in his work. He had often introduced classical details as part of the mix, as we have seen in the interiors of Marsh Court. In lockdown during the Covid pandemic, the American architect Oliver Cope put his time to good use by studying the façades of Lutyens's Arts and Crafts country houses. He found that they were composed according to simple geometrical principles – the almost inevitable result for an architect whose basic tools were T-square, set square and compass.

Furthermore, some of his contemporaries had discovered Wren, Lutyens's great hero and apparent mentor in Classicism, many years before. In 1889, the Scottish architect John Brydon had given a lecture which identified the Early English Renaissance – the century that ended with the death of Wren in 1723 – as having furnished 'the national style': a specifically English form of Classicism which provided 'a great mine of artistic wealth open to all who have eyes to see, hearts to appreciate, and understanding to apply to the

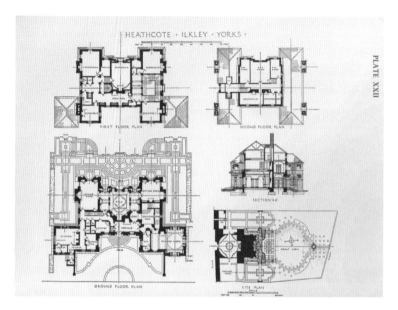

HEATHCOTE · ILKLEY · YORKS ·

Externally, Heathcote may be symmetrical but the plan remains as Picturesque as an Arts and Crafts building. There is no view through the house from front door to garden: instead the visitor follows a circuitous route before the big reveal.

With its mustard-coloured walls and red tiled roof, Heathcote must have astounded the Hemingways' neighbours in Ilkley. Lutyens's inspiration is not Wren but the Porta Palio gate in the city walls of Verona by the Mannerist architect Sanmicheli.

necessities of our day'.[2] Numerous Edwardian town halls, commercial buildings and the new palaces for bureaucrats in Whitehall were derived from it. What was new about Lutyens was the discipline. His contemporaries were influenced – as in his way, Lutyens himself was – by the 'anything goes' approach of the Edwardian Freestyle. This represented a loosening of the corsets after the stern stylistic rectitude of the Gothic Revival, with its moral abhorrence of the Classical. Freestyle architects saw themselves as having moved beyond the style wars; they picked what they liked from wherever they found it, incorporating apparently incompatible ideas and motifs in the same building. This produced a crop of jolly libraries, public baths and temperance billiard halls. Its influence was less positive on the public architecture that goes by the name of Edwardian Baroque. Huge in scale but unconstrained by the rules that guided architects in the seventeenth century, it can give a strong impression of having eaten too much rich food, and bulging in the wrong places. Domes proliferate: they were no longer feared for their contaminating association with Roman Catholicism. So does sculpture, which could be of a high standard. Architects such as John Belcher sought to achieve a marriage between architecture and sculpture in works such as the Institute of Chartered Surveyors Building on Moorgate: the union was an ideal of the Art Workers' Guild. Edwardian Baroque was often better inside than out, overpowering visitors with operatic staircases lined with marbles of many colours. This was a long way from Lutyens's concept of the Renaissance.

There was another strand to the story, however. For some time, the Arts and Crafts Movement, originally medieval in inspiration, had been exploring a style of red brick, hipped roofs, sash windows, tall chimneys and dormers. This was given a fillip by John Belcher and Mervyn Macartney whose *Later Renaissance Architecture in England* had been published in 1901. The book described what we would now call the Baroque era, still craftsman-built but whose well-lit, regularly proportioned rooms with their tall ceilings provided a more popular example to follow than the small windows and cubbyhole-like spaces of the earlier period. This sort of architecture was also less trouble to design. It suited the taste for a quieter domestic style that took hold of the better architects after 1900. The epithet used by Lawrence Weaver of the English Renaissance style of Ardenrun Place, Surrey, begun by Ernest Newton in 1906, was 'extraordinarily ordinary'.[3] Were it possible to see Ardenrun today – it burnt down in 1933 – we might not come to quite this judgment, not least because of the quality of the craftsmanship. But for a large house created for the banker H. H. Konig it lacked the look-on-my-works-and-despair quality of a big house of a generation before.

Heathcote was not reticent. One of the surprises of visiting it in person, should one have only seen the black-and-white photographs in *Country Life*, is the colour. The coarse local stone of the walls is practically mustard, the clay tiles of the roof bright orangey red; there is a suggestion of the racegoer in a loud check suit. This must have been quite something for the Hemingways' former neighbours around The Grove, let alone those of Canal Road, Bradford. But Lutyens was pulling no punches. Three years before he had described his ambition in a letter to Baker:

In architecture, Palladio is the game. It is so big – few appreciate it now and it requires considerable training to value and realise it. The way Wren handled it was marvellous. To the average man it is dry bones but under the mind of Wren it glows, and the stiff materials become as plastic clay ... It is a game that never deceives, dodges never disguises. It means hard thought all through – if it is laboured it fails. There is no fluke that helps it – the very what one might call the machinery of it makes it impossible except in the hands of a Jones or a Wren. So, it is a big game, a high game, a game that [Alfred] Stevens played well as an artist should – tho' he never touched Wren.

Strangely, the inspiration of Heathcote was not Wren but the sixteenth-century Venetian Mannerist architect Michele Sanmicheli – specifically his gate in the walls of Verona known as the Porta Palio. This gave the clue as to how he could achieve a greater grandeur in the façades than the room heights would have permitted. The cornice of the Doric order does not reflect the internal form of the building – a mismatch that a more academic Classicist would have regarded as a solecism. Beneath the cornice is rustication, which merges with the Doric pilasters: a visual caprice which Lutyens repeated in later buildings. The vigorous projections and recessions of the façade have the plasticity of sculpture. Lutyens's assurance is breath-taking. Having gone into bat against the cricket-playing Baker, he hit the ball into the stands.

As Lutyens declared to his friend and rival, work of this kind requires the 'hard labour' of intense application and thought – especially in Britain, where architectural education was haphazard. In France, the École des Beaux-Arts instilled the principles of Classical design in its students through a vigorous method, which led them to produce ravishing architectural drawings of capitals and other details. Only a few British architects attended it; most picked up their Classical knowledge in the offices of older architects who themselves had not been Classically trained. Lutyens barely even had that level of training. Yet his Wrennaissance was truly a Renaissance: the rebirth of a style that had, for the most part in Britain, lost its intellectual rigour. Heathcote restored it.

Not having been drilled in the doctrine of the Beaux-Arts, Lutyens took an individual approach to planning. Except in the Viceroy's House, which was of a different size from his other projects, he never unfolds his houses in an obvious way. Classicism dictates symmetry; there are strict axes from front to back and side to side. This usually means a visitor can walk in a straight line from the front door to the garden. A Lutyens house, by contrast, is a journey, a succession of reveals – which usually begins before the house has even been reached; the driveway will take circuitous route, as at Marsh Court, or the entrance will be made through an archway, concealing the house until the last moment – see Great Maytham, Plumpton Place, Berrydown and The Salutation. At Heathcote, the front door does not give into the centre of an entrance hall, as you would expect. Instead, the hall has been placed asymmetrically, with the front door at one end. Similarly, the drawing room in the centre of the garden front is only revealed after a circuitous route (or choice of routes), leading to pairs of doors that are again not axially placed but stand at either end. It is as though Lutyens wants to build the quirkiness of old country houses that have grown organically into one that is both new and Classical.

Hemingway had never encountered anyone like Lutyens before. By now, however, Lutyens had considerable experience of clients and could play him like a trout on the River Test. 'He didn't know how to spend his money until he met me,' he laughed. His behaviour was outrageous. When Hemingway told him that he did not want a black staircase but an oak one, Lutyens said: 'What a pity.' Later, he arrived to find that a black marble staircase of the most sumptuous kind had been constructed. 'I told you I didn't want a marble staircase,' he complained.

'I know,' replied Lutyens, 'and I said: "What a pity" didn't I?'

Despite the provenance (Lutyens's daughter, Mary) I cannot quite believe this story, but why spoil a good joke? It has a poetic truth. Hemingway was rinsed. Even so he must have enjoyed the relationship at some level. Far from dismissing his architect, Hemingway seems to have accepted that the only thing to do was to give him a free hand – the decoration of the house was left entirely to Lutyens.

Another of Sanmicheli's Verona gates – Porta San Zeno – provided the crib for the richly architectural branch building that Lutyens designed for the Midland Bank on Piccadilly. The source is doubly remarkable, because the bank (now a shop and cocktail bar for the publishers Assouline) stands next to the Wren church of

The owner of Heathcote supposedly wanted a wooden staircase but Lutyens substituted a marble one while he was away. The magnificence of this triple height space must have raised eyebrows in Ilkley.

St James's, Piccadilly. St James's is built of tawny brick; the brick of the Midland Bank – such as it shows between the elaborate stone dressings – is of a brighter red. The Wrenaissance did not take itself too literally.

'I marvel at San Michele [sic], though I have only seen photos and drawings,' wrote Lutyens – which raises the question of how he knew of the work; he did not get to Italy until 1909 and even then did not visit Verona. Sanmicheli himself did not publish his designs in a book. Presumably Lutyens had studied Ferdinando Albertolli's *Porte di Città e Fortezze Depositi Sepolcrali ed Altre Principali Fabbriche Pubbliche e Private di Michele Sammicheli Veronese*. Lutyens could have found it in the library of the Royal Institute of British Architects. Probably it was also one of the books circulated among the members of the Foreign Architectural Book Society (F.A.B.S.) to which Lutyens belonged, dining with them or visiting old buildings. 'A sumptuous tea and then whiskey', was his happy comment after one outing.

The site chosen for the *Country Life* office was not in the wilds of the country but Tavistock Street, Covent Garden. But Covent Garden then served as a vegetable and flower market, which made it as rural as it was possible to get in the great, smog-bound imperial metropolis of London. Nor did Lutyens's design require him to travel, even in imagination: here was the true Wren-based Wrenaissance, an essence of Hampton Court to dignify a street whose gutters were rarely free from the odd cabbage, fallen from a porter's barrow. Except that this is no copy of Wren. With astonishing bravura, Lutyens has taken the elements of Wren's style and done something that Charles II's architect did not. Due to the narrowness of the street, this was never a building that could be seen from a distance. The upper floors could not be much studied without a crick in the neck. The drama is therefore concentrated at street and mezzanine level, unified by rusticated bands of Portland

The *Country Life* building in Covent Garden, 1904, is an extraordinarily assured first outing in Classicism. Lutyens took Wren's Hampton Court as his theme but does not copy; there is nothing in Wren's oeuvre exactly like the doorcase with segmental pediment embracing the mezzanine.

stone; the mezzanine windows are borrowed from Hampton Court but not the great segmental pediment which you assume shelters the front door – but no, actually it embraces a mezzanine window: the front door is far below it. The splendid pediment, rising from banks of Corinthian pilasters, gives the impression that, far from being a magazine office, this is a town palace for giants. Richness is heaped on richness, but tied together with such a thorough understanding of the classical rulebook that it never runs to fat.

There is no doorcase of this kind in Wren's oeuvre. Whisper it only, but the inspiration may have been even closer to home than Hampton Court. In 1904, the year before Hudson commissioned

Lutyens to do the *Country Life* office, Horace Field's design for an office for the North Eastern Railway at 4 Cowley Street, Westminster, was both published in *The Builder* and exhibited at the Royal Academy.[4] Field was an Arts and Crafts architect who designed branches for Lloyds Bank across Britain in a brick seventeenth-century style and co-wrote (with his former assistant, Michael Bunney) the widely read *English Domestic Architecture of the XVII and XVIII Centuries*, published in 1905. William and Mary style, segmental pediment, a central window with volutes at the bottom of the frame, the technical detail of dosserets above the capitals of the pilasters to either side of the door … Lutyens would certainly have been aware of the design when he was at work on the *Country Life* building and the similarities are telling. Classicism was in the air. Lutyens picked up ideas where he could find them, usually developing those which came from contemporary sources with a panache that exceeds the original.

The *Country Life* building was a London project. It provided a stepping stone to the big public commissions that are any architect's goal. Soon enough, he was invited to enter the competition for County Hall, home of the London County Council, overlooking the Thames: Lutyens put in a great deal of work on his unsuccessful entry, based on Wren's buildings at Greenwich. When Lutyens did not get the job, he raged against fate. But within six years he had obtained the biggest commission anyone could have wished for in the Viceroy's House and the imperial capital of New Delhi. Before that there was another house to build: Castle Drogo.

SEVEN

INDESTRUCTIBLE, SEVERE AND MAGNIFICENT

Castle Drogo, Devon 1910–30

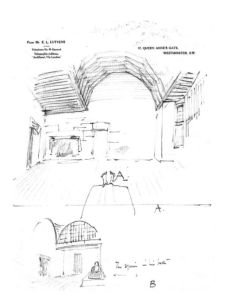

'The squire in his bath': a doodle illustrating Julius Drewe's monumental bathroom at Castle Drogo, complete with Diocletian window in homage to the Baths of Ancient Rome. For added drama the approach to the bath was made past a giant Tuscan column made of wood. The upper part of the sheet shows Drewe's dressing room, which, as can be seen from the feet appearing at the end of the bedclothes, contained a bed. It is also called the Ship Room from a wooden ceiling resembling an inverted hull. (These rooms appear in the centre of the top plan on page 126.)

T HERE WAS ONLY ONE ARCHITECT WHO COULD design a castle and that was Lutyens. Such was the opinion of *Country Life* when Julius Drewe, owner of a large chain of grocery shops, consulted them on his intention to build Castle Drogo. When Drewe wrote Ned 'a nice and exciting letter' in August 1910, the gift horse was looked in the mouth. 'Only I do wish he didn't want a castle but just a delicious lovable house with plenty of good large rooms in it,' he told Emily. The budget was £50,000 plus £10,000 for the garden.

> I suppose £60,000 sounds a lot to you but I don't know what it means. If I look at Westminster Abbey it is an absurd – trivial amount. If I look at a dear little old world two roomed cottage it merely looks a vast and unmanageable amount.

For Lutyens to be measuring the funds available against the cost of building Westminster Abbey, however small they would have been for the purpose, shows that his ambition had risen to the construction of great monumental projects. Viewed as a country house, Drogo would be one of them: not a building to rival the Abbey but an epic work, of greater imagination than any other house of its age. And it was a stepping-stone to the great, more abstract works of the second half of his career. Drogo raised Lutyens's game.

On a sunny spring day, Castle Drogo, on its bluff overlooking the wilds of Dartmoor, could fairly be described as sparkling. The complex angles of the stone are as sharp as when the masons cut them one hundred years ago: of course they always have been – the building is made of granite. The surprise is that the stone itself was shown to have changed colour when it was cleaned as part of the National Trust's nine-year restoration. Before, a century of exposure to the elements had turned it to a dark and gloomy grey, due to the incrustation of lichens that had built up. While lichens may be friends to the appearance of stonework in other places, such as the Cotswolds, here they masked the beauty of the underlying material: now that they have been removed we see blocks of subtly varying shades, predominantly silvery grey but scattered with accents of brown, charcoal and pink. Alas, this will change over the coming

Castle Drogo, built to overlook the wilds of Dartmoor, was intended to have been three times the size: the gravel entrance forecourt stands on the foundations laid for the great hall. The mainly silvery granite has subtle variations in colour.

Castle as sculpture. Following the reduction in scale, Drogo is now most memorable for circulation spaces such as this staircase. The ceiling height remains the same while the stairs descend. The portrait shows Frances Drewe, the owner's wife.

decades as the lichens resume their reign. But for the time being, it is possible to see this gargantuan Edwardian caprice with the eyes of its creators.

Drewe wanted a castle of romance: he got one that has only minimal crenellation, no machicolation – not even suits of armour in the hall or trophies of arms on the staircase, which were so sought after in the salerooms. Lutyens penetrated to the essence of castleness, abstracted what he found and used it to his own expressive purpose, much as he did Classicism. It is not the living rooms that we remember from Drogo, for they are conventional, but the circulation spaces: the passageways and staircases with their exciting if inconvenient changes of level – a truly castle-like feature which he had internalised from Lindisfarne and Lambay. The same ceiling height is maintained throughout the length of the main staircase, so that it is 13ft at the top and 27ft at the bottom. We are left with the sense that Drogo is a gigantic piece of sculpture, whose spatial drama amazes the visitor at every turn.

Drewe's full-length portrait hangs on the staircase. It shows him in Scotland, dressed in tweeds, with an enormous salmon at his feet; possibly he is wearing the favourite cap to which a curtain-like flap could be attached by poppers, fastening under the chin. At other times, he wore a suit, discarding the matching waistcoat (he had a drawer of unworn waistcoats) in favour of a light-coloured one, his off-white tie fastened with a diamond pin. The son of a clergyman, he got his first job through an uncle, the Peek of the tea importers Francis Peek and Winch, one of whose family also founded Peek Freans biscuits. This gave Drewe the opportunity to visit China, Japan and San Francisco as a tea buyer. By twenty-seven, he was frustrated with his position and started a chain of Willow Pattern Tea Stores, largely selling tea. This was followed by the Home and Colonial Stores – its name inspired by a sister who was soliciting donations to a missionary society called the Home and Colonial

Training Establishment. In 1903 it had over 500 outlets. By that time, however, Drewe had already made enough money to retire from active participation in the firm, which he did at the age of thirty-three. He never mentioned trade again.

The castle archive contains a typescript memoir by Adrian Francis Drewe, Julius's grandson, who says that Drewe made up his mind instantly, never changed it, and usually got – as in the case of his castle – what he wanted. Sitting in a hotel in Brighton one day, he saw a tall, slender, blue-eyed eighteen-year-old girl called Frances Richardson walk in. 'That's the girl I'm going to marry,' he said, turning to an associate. He did marry her and, according to a reminiscence by his daughter Frances, 'they were never apart at any time.'[1] The Drews, as they then were, enjoyed a happy family life at Wadhurst Park, in East Sussex, previously home to the Murietta brothers – bankers who failed to weather the Baring Crisis of 1890. The house came with all the Muriettas' furniture, much of which is now at Drogo. On Sundays, chapel was central to the day, with the evangelical Julius himself teaching in the Sunday school.

A warm-hearted husband, prone to practical jokes and generous to charities, he was adored by his five children whose musical talents meant that they could practically form their own orchestra. But like some other self-made men, he developed an *idée fixe* about his lineage. In this he was encouraged by his brother Willie, a barrister. Research commissioned from Culleton's Heraldic Office and Reference Library postulated a descent from the Drogo who accompanied William the Conqueror in 1066, whose descendant Drogo de Teign gave his name to Drewsteignton. In 1903, Willie persuaded Julius to buy most of the village of Broadhembury in Devon, along with some land and portraits, previously belonging to the Drewe family of The Grange, the last of whom had died. Later he would 'restore' his name from Drew to Drewe to cement the connection. Strangely, he stopped short of acquiring The Grange itself but created another dwelling called Culverhayes from a farmhouse; perhaps his hands were already full at Wadhurst, or perhaps the idea of Drogo had taken shape.

Blissful at Wadhurst, Drewe's family were horrified by the idea of re-establishing themselves in Devon. Lutyens, as we have seen, had reservations of his own – not least because 1910–11 marked, as Christopher Hussey put it, the flood tide of his career. But the romance proved irresistible: he got caught up in the dream, producing dozens of sketches using his favourite worm's eye view to make the most of the drama, and rearranging pepper and salt pots when eating with the Drewes to illustrate his latest ideas. The inspiration was not wholly medieval. Just as the design of Drogo was starting, Lutyens's friend Cecil Baring took him to stay with his Mildmay cousins at Mothecombe in Devon. From there he showed him Richard Norman Shaw's Flete – '*awfully nouveau riche,*' was Lutyens's verdict: over-elaborate and 'agog with patterns, a pity'. But that did not stop him from borrowing the idea of a rugged tower rising sheer and almost without mouldings.

Drewe wanted more than a country house of that kind, and there emerged a gargantuan complex with a gate tower, outer court and splayed wings, which would have dominated the ridge on which it was placed with buildings as big as those of medieval castle like Richmond in Yorkshire. Believing her father to be a 'very wonderful person', Frances did not think that it was so very extraordinary for the time.

> The conception of 1910 was an eminently practical one … His plan was to build his castle in form and substance indestructible, severe and magnificent, yet furnished inside with every modern amenity so as to provide an extremely comfortable home. A large staff would be needed, but that was no problem in those days; ample electricity was provided by a large turbine

installation built in conjunction with a weir on the river Teign below; a complete central heating system was installed which admittedly consumed a ton of coke a day, but with prices then prevailing that was no problem either; underground storage was provided for a year's supply. Externally the walls and roof were of solid granite, the windows all bronze casements and the only painting was to the flagstaff! Inside the walls were either natural granite, white plaster, panelled or hung with tapestries, the sole exception being the drawing room where the panelling was painted. Maintenance therefore was intended to be negligible and when the central heating was on the building acted like a gigantic heat storage unit, keeping the whole place at a comfortable and uniform temperature.

Admittedly it would be 'a mammoth enterprise' but the cost, at the prices of the day, could have been easily absorbed 'without any serious depletion of resources'. According to a plan in the RIBA Drawings Collection, this castle would have made spectacular use of the falling site to provide an enfilade of three enormous rooms – dining room, great hall and drawing room – looking south. There was to have been a large laboratory – did Drewe have scientific interests? – between an internal court and a Wagnerian great hall with two fireplaces each 12ft wide.

This was not to be. The 1,200 or so plans and drawings that are kept at Drogo chart Drewe's retreat. Half the structure was sacrificed in 1912, as surplus to even Drewe's requirements. Lutyens clung to his gate tower and outer court, proposing to join them to the stables: a full-scale mock-up was made out of the wooden shuttering brought onto the site for concrete floors. But the date – 1916 – probably explains why nothing was done. The next year the Drewes' eldest son Adrian, an artillery major, was killed in France, taking the joy out of their lives; thereafter Julius became something

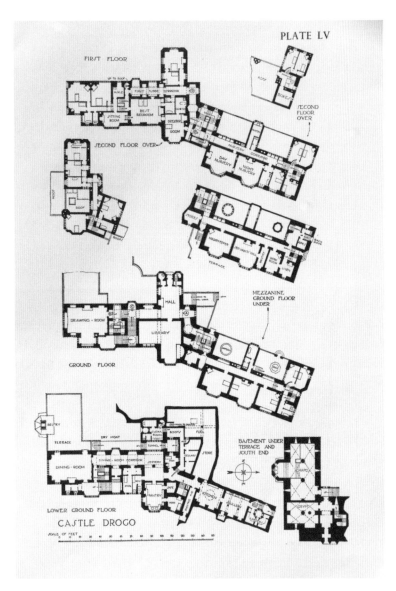

PLATE LV

The plan of Castle Drogo shows the numerous passages and staircases but not the complexity of the spaces, due to the many changes of level which had been a feature of Lindisfarne and Lambay. By contrast, the main rooms are relatively conventional in form.

of a valetudinarian. With taxes and trebled building costs, the post-war years were not a time for building castles. Further contractions were made until the last designs were made for the chapel in 1930. What exists today is a mere third of the size of the original scheme, making its scale pretty much that of Flete.

The new castle made use of a portion that had already been built, but to quite different effect. The double-height dining room was divided horizontally in two, with the drawing room occupying the upper half. This provided rooms of exactly the sort that Lutyens had originally hoped for – large but not Brobdingnagian. A billiard room opens off the library. All these interiors, however, are strangely disproportionate to the element of the house that is now the most memorable: the staircases and hallways. The reductions had made Drogo somewhere that is best experienced as you walk through it, thrilled by the sculptural treatment of the great granite masses and dizzying voids.

The visitor's first view of Drogo, from the north, shows a densely packed cluster of cuboids of different heights. Like a true castle, the windows appear to have been placed haphazardly – a reflection of the changes in floor level that echo Lutyens's previous experience of Lindisfarne and Lambay. The main entrance, to the west, stands at the base of a tower and guarded by a portcullis, originally operated by a geared winch, which the National Trust hopes to restore with an electric motor; octagonal turrets to either side end in battlements and arrow-slits. Strangely, perhaps, other obviously castle-like features, such as machicolation, are kept to a minimum – the battlements only project by matter of inches and there is practically no crenellation, which would have detracted from the play of volumes. Instead Lutyens draws on a repertoire of non-castle forms, such as banks of mullion windows of Elizabethan type (a weak point in the case of attack on a real castle). There are three such banks on the south front, to take advantage of the views down the gorge. The walls are battered – a castle motif – but set between razor-sharp fins that look practically Art Deco. Between the fins the wall surface steps back almost as though it has been carved. Doors disappear into tunnels beneath overscale mouldings that belong more to fireplaces than the outside of a castle. Drogo propelled Lutyens on the journey towards abstraction which ended in the Cenotaph, the Viceroy's House at New Delhi and the largely unbuilt Liverpool Cathedral.

When the client rejected the proposed pitched roof, which would have kept out the weather, preferring a more castle-like flat roof and parapets, Lutyens seized the chance to design an up-and-down puzzle of different geometrical shapes – there are twenty-eight different roofs altogether, reached by stepping from one to the other or by staircases, which sometimes lead to unusable wells just for the fun of it. The size of two football pitches, they make an adventure playground of geometrical shapes, levels and voids, which must have provided a thrilling if sometimes dangerous sequence of secret spaces for Drewe's grandchildren. Old photographs suggest that the roofs were much used as outdoor rooms. After stewing in the Turkish bath (no longer extant), the Drewes would go directly onto the roofs to experience a cooling blast of fresh air from across Dartmoor or the Teign Gorge.[2]

In style, Drogo took its theme from the distant past, but no self-conscious throwback was needed when it came to the granite. The techniques employed by stone masons on Dartmoor had changed little for centuries. This appealed to Lutyens's abiding love of the Arts and Crafts. Admittedly greater attention was given to aesthetic effect than would have been typical in other works. Each course of granite was marked on the architect's scale drawings. Outside, the predominant finish was pitted or 'rustic punched', with the window and door surroundings being more smoothly finished. Originally Lutyens had envisaged that only rough granite would be used, but gave fresh orders on returning to Delhi without asking Drewe. The client exploded when he found out. 'To my mind ... the building should be continued to your pre-Delhian instructions. What might have happened to us if you had also seen the Pyramids as well makes us quake to think about.'

Lutyens had, as ever, faith in his superior judgment. 'The big lumpy blocks are right for the lower courses but quite impossible to carry them up ... it would mean a barbaric building worthy of a small municipal corporation ... I am very keen about your castle and must "fight" you when I KNOW I am right.' He got his way. The exchange raises the interesting possibility of Indian influence on Drogo: it is tempting to think that the schematised vault over the stair shows the influence of the Great Stupa at Sanchi, which Lutyens knew from his work on the Viceroy's House. There is also a sole, mysterious column near the kitchen which seems of Indian form.

Drewe was not the only rich Edwardian to have an eye for a castle. Builders did not generally have to start from scratch, because of the large number of ruins that could be converted to homes, without – in those days – the need to obtain listed building consent. William Waldorf Astor bought Hever Castle in 1903, adding a wing of guest accommodation in the form of a Tudor village on the other side of the moat. In 1913, Colonel Claude Lowther started to restore Herstmonceux; ultimately his work would be completed by Sir Paul Latham twenty years later, but for a short time after 1929 it was owned by Reginald Lawson (who killed himself in the grounds of his other castle, Saltwood, in 1930). Lawson, whose wife came from Texas, belonged to a group of castle enthusiasts with American money. They included Lord Curzon, twice married to Americans, at Bodiam, in Sussex; Lady Baillie, whose father had married a Whitney, at Leeds Castle, in Kent; the mountaineer-cum-art historian, Martin Conway, at Allington Castle, with his first wife Katrina, the daughter of an American railroad magnate; and the American newspaper magnate William Randolph Hearst at St Donat's. Castle owners formed a select club. Drogo was not the only castle to be constructed *de novo*, as can be seen from Amicia de Moubray's *Twentieth Century Castles in Britain*, published in 2013; but it was far and away the most ambitious.

Indeed, Drogo was a project of daunting complexity, requiring scores of workmen over a period of twenty years – four of which coincided with the First World War. It is extraordinary that it was ever finished. In this, the hero of the piece is John Walker, Drewe's agent on site, without whom the castle would not have been built.

A Yorkshireman, Walker had previously been clerk of works at various country houses, including Welbeck Abbey, which, from 1905, was being rebuilt after a fire. He appears at Drogo in 1912 and his work over the next two decades can be followed through the copies of his letters that exist in the Castle. Each time Walker wrote to Drewe, Lutyens or a supplier, he put his freshly hand-written letter in a press which took a faint copy by a chemical reaction on very thin paper – a method that had been used since the mid Victorian period and was being replaced, in the age of the typewriter, by carbon paper. The copies were later bound together in fat letterbooks. There are around 6,000 letters. An early request was to transfer a trap from the Drewes' Sussex home of Wadhurst Park to Devon and buy a pony for it locally. Masons are then recruited at 8½ *d.* per hour for time worked (they had to pay their own railway fares and lodgings). In June Walker was down with what he took to be blood poisoning from the 'bad smells' around the cottage at Drewe's village of Drewsteignton, where he was staying; dustbins were provided for his neighbours to dispose of their rubbish, rather than throwing it on the floor. Happily, he soon recovered. Everything on the estate fell to his care, down to organising the celebrations at Drewsteignton for Adrian Drewe's coming of age and similarly for the election of another Drewe son, Cedric, as an MP.

The quarry was a constant anxiety. The choice had fallen on Blackinstone but the granite blocks were delivered in the wrong sizes, in the wrong order and incorrectly dressed. He fell out with the quarry foreman, a Mr Crabb: when Crabb retired, he wrote to the quarry urging that the job would not be given to Crabb's son, who might be as bad if not worse. He and Lutyens were forced to resort instead to commissioning a series of other quarries alongside Blackinstone, to keep up with demand. There were Merrivale, Pew Tor and Drewe's own small quarry on Whiddon Down. Transporting the blocks by 'motor trolley' from Moretonhampstead station played havoc with the country roads. There were accidents – one man lost part of a thumb – and strikes; away from home, the men needed to be entertained with whist drives and sports days. Driving rain meant days lost. The local council complained that the necessary permissions had not been obtained. Masons and granite cutters could go on strike. When some large boulders were needed to add a rugged look to the base of the walls, it was Walker who had to source them.

Work slowed during the First World War. Drewe encouraged single men to enlist and gave them a bounty that would cover the cost of their kit. When the Devon War Agricultural Committee complained that too many able-bodied men were still at Drogo, Drewe responded that forty had already left to sign up. Several of their names appear on the war memorials of local villages. When in 1917, the Drewes' eldest son Adrian was killed in Flanders, a bronze figure of Victory was commissioned to stand before his portrait, in a shrine-like room full of his possessions. Walker had already closed work on the castle, as he wrote to the sculptor Joseph Armitage, 'until the word peace is said'.

It was Armitage who carved the splendid Venetian-looking lion over the entrance. A member, like Lutyens, of the Art Workers' Guild, his choice has turned out to be highly appropriate, since he also designed the oak-leaf symbol of the National Trust. The Drogo commission, however, was not without incident: two drawings for the lion were rejected, one (at full size) because it had been made too big. These difficulties were overcome and in 1920 the relief was put in place. Other carving was intended for the entrance hall: 'The idea', as Walker put it to Lutyens's assistant John Thomas, 'was to have Lizards & such like things crawling about especially on the stops of chamfers, not crests or Coats of Arms ... I am writing Mr Palliser [another sculptor] who, if he knows about the Small Crawling things, may know how to sketch some designs for Mr Drewe to see.' They were never carried out.[3]

Inside the castle, pale grey granite predominates in the circulation spaces, the rooms being panelled in oak or mahogany, except for the drawing room whose green painted panels have inspired Little Greene to offer a 'Sir Lutyens' Sage' to its range. Being perfectly happy with the furniture at Wadhurst, the Drewes brought it to Drogo. They seem barely to have added to the Muriettas' collection, beyond the Venetian chandelier that they bought on their honeymoon and an elaborate grandfather clock which they saw at the Paris Exhibition. One of the tapestries – presumably a Murietta piece – has been identified as a treasure of previously unnoticed worth: a Char de Triomphe tapestry made for Louis XIV, one of only five in the world. The Drewes did not use their wealth to buy great paintings and the portraits they commissioned are mediocre. Despite having built a castle at great expense, Julius did not fill it with the arms and armour that were then fashionable. Instead the furnishings are conventionally domestic, with rugs on the floor to add a softer note. Drewe was, however, a lover of gadgets, who would put a clockwork bird in a tree to trick his children into thinking the music was birdsong. The dining room had an electric tablecloth so that lamps could be plugged into it wherever needed (the linen was heavily singed as a result). Presumably it was Lutyens who arranged the lighting on the staircase. A ceiling fixture takes the form of a cherub holding light bulbs. Uplighters (which he deplored elsewhere) were hidden behind other cherubs in the niches to the side of the staircase to provide a touch of Art Deco drama. Otherwise, because of the Wadhurst furniture and the castle's reduction in size, the most striking rooms are, curiously, the kitchen and scullery, fitted out by Lutyens with a mortar and pestle fit for a giant.

Lutyens made use of some novel constructional techniques. Disastrously, he employed a new and untried product – asphalt – to seal the roofs and make them watertight (possibly, after the First World War when so much metal was melted down to make armaments, there was a shortage of lead); it failed. And both roofs and floors were made of reinforced concrete, a material more usually associated with the Modern Movement than the work of an arch-traditionalist. Concrete was needed to meet the client Julius Drewe's desire for roofs that were flat, as befitted a castle. If only Lutyens had stuck to the use of pitched roofs, as originally proposed, a deal of trouble would have been avoided.

Wanting a proper castle, Drewe also insisted on solid walls – if not granite all the way through, then with the gap between the two thick outer granite skins packed hard with rubble. This would prove equally unfortunate in the battle against lashing rain. Damp was taking authenticity too far; it might not have mattered so much in the castles of the Middle Ages but unacceptable in one that doubled as an early twentieth-century country house.

At last, in 1925, the family could move into part of the castle. Two years later the furniture and many of the staff from their beloved Wadhurst Park were moved to Devon and the Sussex house sold. However, the castle still needed a chapel. This Lutyens provided in the undercroft that had originally been intended to support the abandoned great hall. It was a typically ingenious solution, which placed the pews and organ from Wadhurst on a higher level than the chancel; the latter was placed in a projection between two of the cyclopean buttresses, where it could be lit both by stained glass, again from Wadhurst, and a concealed window. The congregation looks down from the shadows onto a chancel that is bathed in light. This work was completed in 1930, the year before Drewe's death. The organ is now being restored, thanks to a grant from the Lutyens Trust.

Ominously, in January 1917 Walker had wired the roofers Salter Edwards and Company about a leak in the nursery: the pieces of asphalt had not been properly jointed to one another. Leaks would prove a depressing leitmotif in Drogo's subsequent history. The National Trust was well aware of them when it bravely accepted the family's gift of the castle in 1974, not much more than forty years after its completion. As well as being poorly fitted, the asphalt cracked under the extremes of the Dartmoor weather, which can be baking or freezing according to season. Attempts to mend the problem, by removing the stone flags from the roof and putting down a screed of concrete, did no good. In fact this remedial work destroyed the subtle cambers that had allowed rain water to run into the internal downpipes, its passage slowed by joints between the flags to prevent them from being overwhelmed. In time, the hundreds of glass panes in the windows got loose in their cames as the linseed putty aged, allowing water to get in there too. A major programme of repair in the 1980s failed to solve the problems. From 1996, the firm of Inskip and Jenkins was employed to take a root-and-branch approach, which culminated, in 2013, with a campaign to install a modern waterproofing membrane across all the roofs and undertake forty miles of repointing to take out the sand and cement mortar that had been mistakenly applied under the family ownership and replace it with breathable lime mortar. During this work, the top courses of the walls, to a height of four or five feet, were removed, numbered and placed alongside the drive. All the windows were also removed. Keeping the original glass, the gun-metal window frames were blasted to expunge layers of paint and dirt; the lead cames were replaced, and the glass covered in ultra-violet filters to protect the contents of the castle.

When Lytton Strachey visited Lindisfarne, off the Northumberland coast, he found it uncomfortable. Would the same have been said of Drogo? The chimneys smoked, as Lutyens often did, and water poured in through the walls. But Drewe only stayed there during the summer. In 1919 he bought Kilmorie, a large house in Torquay that he had long coveted and used that for the winter; it was where he died in 1931. If all else failed there was his luxurious steam yacht *Devonia*. As a boy, Adrian Francis Drewe – named after his dead uncle – loved going to sleep in the Tower Room, the highest in the castle, which 'seemed to be miles from anywhere', with the wind 'always whining or screaming … caught perhaps by the sharp angles of the tower or the chimney or whistling under the door.' Drogo was an adventure.

As a solid and indestructible family seat, which would be so soundly built as to require next to no maintenance, Drogo was a failure. In 1916 Basil found that the genealogical research that had so excited his father was largely bogus, undermining the premise on which Drogo was built. Nevertheless, the Castle succeeded in linking the Drewe name forever with Dartmoor, and through the National Trust it will be remembered far into the future. In the Home and Colonial Stores, Julius Drewe had a partner called Musker. His taste was for racehorses, rather than architecture. Today he has been forgotten outside horsey circles. If only he had asked Lutyens to build him a castle.[4]

EIGHT

BYZANTINE-CUM-NEDI

Hampstead Garden Suburb 1908–20

Houses
The Institute
The Free Church
St Jude on the Hill

Perspective design (seventh stage) for the nave of St Jude's, Hampstead Garden Suburb. Lutyens combined the arcades of a conventional parish church with saucer domes from Byzasntium; the timber framework in the aisles, needed to support the enormous, very deep roof, add a barn-like note.

I N August 1907, the Hampstead Garden Suburb
solicitor came, Lutyens wrote, 'to consult me! and their architect came humbly afterwards, rather perturbed, I think.' The
architect was Raymond Unwin, a socialist and vegetarian who was
committed to finding an Arts and Crafts solution to 'the housing
question' – more Emily's sort of person than his own. Since 1903
he and his partner Barry Parker had been planning and designing
Letchworth Garden City; Unwin was now in charge of their office
at Hampstead Garden Suburb, in a house called Wyldes. There
he had been ringing the changes, as Andrew Saint describes, on
'short rows of houses with deep gardens, culs-de-sac, open courts,
advanced and recessed frontage lines, boundary hedges, a varied
geometry of open spaces, "vista-stoppers" for sight-lines, and skewed
road junctions.'[1] To their chagrin, they found that their client, the
formidable Henrietta Barnett, had now gone to Lutyens for the
Central Square. For him it would be a stepping stone to greater
things, being – with Knebworth Garden Village – his only, quite
modest experience of town planning before laying out the imperial
capital of the Raj at New Delhi.

In 1901, Lutyens had designed Greywalls, a holiday home in
Scotland abutting the Muirfield golf course for the Hon. Alfred
Lyttelton, lawyer, sportsman and Liberal Unionist MP. He and his
spiritualist wife Edith, a writer, were members of The Souls. For
all Edith's cleverness, her desire for a fortress with large windows

was a manifest contradiction in terms, and so was the idea that this golfing box should be entered on the sunny south side, leaving the principal rooms to face a dismal North onto the golf course. Lutyens did his best to make sense of the brief, providing a curved front of rough Rattlebag sandstone with pantile roof and casement windows: it provides a sense of protection as well as welcome. The straggling plan (the drawing room is reached by a stalk-like corridor) creates a suntrap that faces east. His efforts were rewarded. Although, because of Edith's fear of railway accidents, the Lytteltons only lived there a few years, before selling to Lutyens's clients at Monkton, Mr and Mrs Willie James, they subsequently asked Ned to design Wittersham House for them in Kent and it was probably Lyttelton, being first the president and then chairman of the Hampstead Garden Suburb Trust Ltd, who got him the job there. Lutyens had long wanted to design a church and this project required two. Central Square would be the site of both an Anglican church and, for other denominations, a Free Church; in different styles, the two would be in dialogue with each other – although it was obvious which was the senior in the relationship, since only the Anglican church, dedicated to St Jude, had a spire. There was no provision for a synagogue although in the course of its history Hampstead Garden Suburb would become home to many Jews.

Barnett, now in her late fifties, typified the zeal of the Edwardian age for reforming itself. Rich from the proceeds of Rowland's Macassar Oil, she married the clergyman Samuel Barnett, later a canon of Westminster Abbey, and lived with him in the vicarage of St Jude's, Whitechapel. It was the Bishop of London's 'worst parish', a criminal congeries of 'wretched streets and foul alleys full of houses that are desolation without and squalor within'. There she threw her energies into the Metropolitan Association for the Befriending of Young Servants (1876), the Children's Country Holiday Fund (1884), the State Children's Association (1896)

Lutyens was commissioned to design Central Square, with (left to right) terraces of houses, the Free Church, the Institute and St Jude's church, in 1907. Although relatively modest, it was his most prominent essay in town planning before New Delhi.

and, from 1884, the University Settlement in East London, better known as Toynbee Hall – a mission where recently graduated university men could live, opening their minds and culture to the poor. Toynbee Hall was followed in 1901 by the Whitechapel Art Gallery, which brought Art to the East End – in a building that was itself an Art Nouveau symbol of rebirth: Harrison Townsend's façade was covered in a filigree of carved vegetation, whose fronds seem on the point of breaking free of the stone. But little real improvement could be made to the Barnetts' Whitechapel without addressing the 'housing question' – the need to rebuild London's slums.

The couple pictured to themselves a different, ideal kind of community, based on the neighbourliness of the English village or market town. The impetus to create one came in 1896, when a Northern Line tube station was proposed for Golders Green.

The Barnetts had a house in Hampstead and foresaw that the underground would trail bricks and mortar in its wake, despoiling what was then still farmland, north of the Heath. Having worked with the social reformer Octavia Hill, co-founder of the National Trust and a champion of the Commons Registration movement, Henrietta set about preserving a northward extension of the heath. These eight acres of open ground would become the lung of a 'garden suburb for all classes', built on the surrounding land. If North Hampstead had to be developed, she would see that it was developed properly.

A picture gallery, bandstand, refreshment rooms, ponds for paddling and sailing, barns for tools, and tenements for the old – such facilities, marked on the map that Unwin drew for the new settlement, show the utopian character of the enterprise. Houses were placed so that none could spoil the outlook of another. Plots were divided by hedges and trellis rather than walls. Old trees were preserved, along with two whole woods. Baillie Scott's Waterlow Court of 1909 sought to answer the problem of single working women who were too hard up to keep house for themselves, which in the Edwardian age meant employing servants; they could enjoy a communal dining room and lounges, as well as a lawn enclosed by a cloister. While the sky would, in Barnett's words, 'flame forth in uninterrupted glory' over the entire scene, the architectural and spiritual focus would be the church of St Jude, dedicated to the same saint as Canon Barnett's church in the East End.

Barnett recalled prospecting for the Central Square with the Hampstead Garden Suburb Trust's first chairman Lord Crewe. They scrambled across rough heathland and hedges until they 'reached the central hill. "This is the highest place, and here we will have the houses for worship and for learning," I said; and here they stand.'[2] The house for learning was the Institute, which emerged as a complex, even perverse piece of rule-breaking Mannerism, in red and grey brick. It was intended, as Barnett put it, 'to help the poor out of poverty by education', by providing self-improvement for adults. To create a plateau on which the two churches and the Institute could stand, the top of the hill was levelled, perhaps preparing Lutyens's mind for similar works that would be undertaken, on a greater scale, on Raisina Hill in New Delhi.

Lutyens's idea of relating architecture to its surroundings could hardly have been more different from Parker and Unwin's Arts and Crafts Picturesque, or the Barnetts' dreams of the rural village. Having discovered Wren, he warmed increasingly to the grandeur of Greenwich – the basis for his LCC competition design – and the avenues and geometry of Wren's unrealised plan to rebuild London after the Great Fire. Unwin had imagined that the heart of Hampstead Garden Suburb would be akin to a village green. By contrast, Lutyens's Central Square would be a big formal space, much like a large London square except that one side would be open to the view. On three sides would be terraces surrounding a big rectangle of grass, approached axially by avenues. This idea was diluted by the omission of some of the houses, and the square was perhaps too big to feel as enclosed as Lutyens intended; certainly today the handsome trees that have been allowed to grow tall and bushy fight against it; Lutyens would have preferred avenues clipped in the French manner. However, Barnett was happy to accept that the layout of paths, trees and beds should conform to his desire for straight lines intersecting at right angles. As she remembered in 1928:

> Curly-shaped beds would not harmonise with the severe lines of the buildings, and unkempt grass would woo noisy boys. But as he left for Marseilles for Delhi, Sir Edwin [Lutyens was knighted in 1919] scrambled off his ideas, just put on rough paper, but as anyone can now see, perfect in proportion and meeting present-day uses.[3]

Drawing of 1910 for Central Square, Hampstead Garden Suburb, which Lutyens conceived as a London square. However, the scale of the open space was too big to create much sense of enclosure and, as can be seen here, the ground fell away to one side.

It was always intended that the churches would occupy different ends of the Square. Between them, on the east side, would be the Institute, flanked by terraces of houses to enclose the space. The open view to the west would make the most of the proximity of the heath – appearing, as it had done to John Constable ninety years before, as a piece of open countryside around which the metropolis would soon spread on all sides.

From the beginning, Barnett envisaged St Jude's as a country church with a spire. Lutyens's design of 1908 provided an Italian scheme with a loggia opening onto the square, with a tall tower derived from the Campanile of St Mark's Square in Venice; to either side, linked by a triumphal arch, were terraces that recall the Place des Vosges in Paris or Inigo Jones's Covent Garden Piazza. Nothing could have been more alien to Barnett's villagey idea. Lutyens was scathing of her aesthetic views. 'A nice woman,' was how Lutyens described her to his wife, 'but proud of being a philistine – has no idea much beyond a window box full of geraniums, calceolarias and lobelias, over which you can see a goose on a green.' The design was revised in a style that Lutyens described as Romantic Byzantine-cum-Nedi; but Barnett was obdurate in wanting Gothic. Lutyens

submitted to the yoke. The new design had a pitched roof and gables; a tower arose over the central crossing and on top of it was a spire.

Although the compromise was not what he would have wished, it became a typical Lutyens synthesis of disparate influences: there are no pointed arches, only round-headed ones; the grey brick with orangey red facings suggests the age of William and Mary, not the immemorial Middle Ages; stylised pilasters flank the larger windows; and he succeeded in keeping a Byzantine interior of red brick, barrel vaults and flat domes, in the spirit of John Francis Bentley's astounding Westminster Cathedral, opened in 1903. There was one more fight to come: although Anglican St Jude's would be the spiritual heart of the community, Barnett feared it would overpower the surrounding houses. Lutyens's solution was to lower the line of the eaves in line with the domestic architecture. This produced an immense sweep of roof with dormers poking out of it, a Surrey cottage theme not usually seen on churches. It adds to the Mannerist tension of the result and caused the arcades of the interior to be reinforced with timber beams and king posts. 'It is a beautiful design that Mr Lutyens has made,' said Barnett, seemingly oblivious of the trouble she had caused, as she turned the first sod in 1909. She later recalled the 'provocative witty poetic' letter that Lutyens wrote to the Barnetts on its completion in 1913.

> I want you both to write something to be placed at the top of the spire of St Jude's Church. The Canon is to write a 'Message to the future,' and you are to say, 'I, even I, by my indomitable will have built what you see all around you.'[4]

Once a battle had been fought, Henrietta Barnett was able to forget the wrangles that had been involved and accept the outcome, almost as though it had been divinely ordained. She may not even have noticed the distress she was causing to Lutyens. To him it was torture.

With its tall spire, St Jude's may the more visible of the two churches, but the Free Church is the more consistent composition: low-domed and truly Byzantine-cum-Nedi. The interior is, writes Mervyn Miller, 'a calm unadorned statement of Lutyens's favourite Tuscan order. All seems sweetness and light in contrast to the *chiaroscuro* of St Jude's.'[5] Of the houses, only the west side of North Square was built (externally) to Lutyens's design: a triumphal arch gives onto a twitten, as the hedge-lined alleyways are known. But he was also responsible for the west side of Erskine Hill, one of the approaches to the Square, and here his genius shines forth in his response to the gradient. Houses of different sizes and set variously up the slope are bound together visually by a white cornice, which remains at the same height throughout the composition, though appearing at different positions on the façades.

Alfred Lyttelton likened Hampstead Garden Suburb to a medieval village, but the inhabitants had acquired some of the Barnetts' campaigning vigour; they were not prepared to take their serfdom lying down. Against Barnett's wishes, they formed a Residents'

Association. The Suburb's rents were not cheap for a family on artisan wages, nor were Parker and Unwin's Arts and Crafts houses wholly convenient for those who retained bulky Victorian furniture from previous dwellings and could not afford the arty built-in pieces that went with the look; gas lighting, provided throughout the Suburb, was progressive, but another expense. What rankled most of all was the paternalistic Barnett-knows-best attitude of the Trust. Lutyens may have been making a sly joke at Henrietta Barnett's expense where, after her death in 1936, he designed her memorial in the form of a crown.

For Unwin, Hampstead Garden Suburb was followed by an influential career in workers' housing, whether for the Ministry of Munitions during the First World War, on the Tudor Walters Committee looking into council housing which reported in 1918, or at the newly formed Ministry of Health. It was an obvious progression, developing the social agenda of Letchworth and Hampstead. By contrast, Lutyens went on to build great set pieces of architecture and lay out New Delhi, works on a quite different scale from his contribution to Barnett's model community. Yet Hampstead Garden Suburb helped to set him too on the path to greatness. He had to manage a considerable volume of sometimes tiresome work, attending committees and countersigning all Unwin's drawings (as Unwin did his). And for once, he did not always get his own way. Barnett was the grit in the oyster that resulted in the architectural pearl of St Jude's. Lutyens's work in India would be forged in the heat of debate, some of it acrimonious. The challenge inspired him to create both a new Classical language and, in the Viceroy's House, one of the greatest monuments of the age.

NINE

WREN COULD
NEVER HAVE
DONE THIS

New Delhi City Plan 1912–30

The Viceroy's House (now Rashtrapati Bhavan) 1912

Members of the Delhi Town Planning Committee attempt to scale an elephant. Lutyens is shown as having stayed on the ground for the moment, although he wrote to Emily that 'we had a very long morning and went miles on the top of this fearful and beloved creature'.

WHILE ST JUDE'S WAS STILL BEING BUILT, Lutyens was commissioned to design the British Pavilion for the International Exhibition of Art in 1911, later to be rebuilt as the British School at Rome. The requirement was specific; it was to be a replica of the upper tier of the west front of St Paul's Cathedral. This chimed with Lutyens's love of Wren, although it also showed how far Wren was generally in the air – for years he had been popularly regarded as the supreme British architect, whose achievement could stand comparison with the greatest architects of the Italian Renaissance to be seen in the Eternal City. In the event Lutyens found he could not simply copy the crib he had been given: he had to reinvent the Classical vocabulary to make it work on a reduced scale, on a building (barely more than a façade) of only one storey. This relatively minor commission was, like Hampstead Garden Suburb, a learning experience. Just as the Suburb had introduced him to Classical town planning, albeit on a modest scale, the British Pavilion at Rome made him concentrate even more closely on the primacy of Wren. Very soon, these grain-like seeds grew into the mustard tree of the new imperial capital of the Raj at New Delhi, focused on the palace for the king-emperor's personal representative, the viceroy. The majesty of the result overwhelmed Edward Hudson, when he saw it in 1928: 'Poor old Christopher Wren,' he said through tears of emotion, 'he could never have done this.' Was this a random compliment? It was well-chosen if so. Lutyens was pitting himself against the greatest architect that Britain had produced, and the early twentieth-century Raj against the Age of the Baroque.

The idea that the imperial capital of India should move from Calcutta to Delhi originated from a small circle around George V. The king-emperor's personal involvement in the project was a significant factor in its success. He himself proposed that he should appear – the first monarch to do so in person – at the Durbar held to announce his succession to the throne. Durbar means assembly; the 'Britishers' called three of them, to announce great imperial events. The 1877 Durbar told the gathered princes and maharajahs that Queen Victoria was now their empress. In 1903, when Lord Curzon was viceroy, the Durbar celebrated the accession of Edward VII. Hyperbolically, the Delhi Durbar of 1911 was described by someone who attended it as 'probably the most magnificent and dazzling spectacle of its kind that the eye of mortal has ever beheld'.[1] In truth, it was somewhat less splendid than Curzon's Durbar, since some of the maharajahs preferred luxurious motor cars to elephants and swarms of picturesque retainers in chain armour and nodding plumes. Nevertheless, eighty thousand Indian potentates and representatives of British India and the princely states were received by the king and queen, and duly astounded when the king announced that the capital would be relocated.

There were moments in Delhi's past that the British did not want to relive. In 1857 it had witnessed a bad episode in what is now sometimes known as India's First War of Independence, but which the Raj called the Indian Mutiny. The rebels massacred all the Europeans that they could find, and it was touch-and-go whether the East India Company's forces, which attempted to besiege the city, would retake it. This near-disaster still pained and horrified the British administration, and it was no coincidence that the Durbar site occupied part of the ridge on which the besieging army had been camped: homage was done to the Empire on the very spot where it had suffered its worst challenge. Would the building of a new capital exorcise the bad spirits?

In London, Curzon was among those who thought not. The cost would be unnecessary and ruinous. But Curzon was no longer viceroy; since 1910 that role had been occupied by Lord Hardinge who believed, optimistically, that the cost 'need not necessarily be formidable' since a million pounds sterling could be found out of revenue for two years without difficulty. This would prove a hopeless underestimate of the budget, which kept rising, only in part due to the First World War. In a country that had been unified by the railway system, Delhi's strategic location – equidistant from Calcutta, Bombay and Karachi – gave it an irresistible advantage.

A committee of three was appointed to draw up a plan.

In hindsight, it might seem obvious that Lutyens would be on it. He was the pre-eminent country-house architect of his generation. His style had evolved from the lyricism and nostalgia of the Surrey Hills to the monumentality of the High Game. He had not won the competition for the London County Council building but his entry showed that he had thought in detail about the organisation of large buildings. But he was not the only successful architect in the game and others (Parker and Unwin, Adshead and Ramsey) had more relevant experience in laying out towns. Apt to be pigeonholed as a country-house specialist, Lutyens had acquired a reputation for being expensive, and he had no experience of dealing with committees operating to budgets that they were not able to alter without reference to higher authorities. If anything, the cards were stacked against him. But he knew how to lobby for work and had made important friends. The support of the newly elevated Marquess of Crewe, who had been chairman of the Hampstead Garden Suburb Trust and was now Secretary of State for India, proved decisive.

On Crewe's suggestion, Captain George Swinton was appointed to chair the committee. Swinton was not an architect but the chairman of the London County Council, founded in 1889 to transform the richest city in the world into a capital that would rank alongside Paris, Berlin, Vienna and the new cities of the United States. Although the 'London of to-day' was 'no longer merely the capital of Great Britain and Ireland', but 'the natural centre of the Anglo-Saxon world – aye, it is its very prototype,' according to the German explorer Dr Carl Peters, and 'the mighty pump, through whose suction pipes British capitalism penetrates into every single country of our planet',[2] its appearance and amenity hardly reflected its role. Thoroughfares that in some cases still followed the medieval street plan were too narrow for the number of horse-drawn hackney cabs using them, let alone the motor car. Projects such as the Strand Improvement Scheme, which widened the Strand and created the Aldwych and Kingsway, served the double purpose of providing a grand ceremonial route (linked, via Sir Aston Webb's Admiralty Arch, to the new Mall, culminating in a 'rond-point' or roundabout in front of Buckingham Palace) and eliminating some notorious slums that were demolished to make way for them. The third member was the 'apple-shaped' engineer, John A. Brodie, described by Lutyens as 'a dear broad matter-of-fact Midland middle-class thing'. He got on well with him.

Lutyens asked that his old friend Herbert Baker – not yet viewed as a dangerous rival – should be appointed to assist him. Although Baker was by far the better qualified for the position of the two, his work, which included the design of the parliament buildings in South Africa's new capital of Pretoria, had almost all been in that country, far from Britain and therefore little known, and also, for reasons of national snobbery, undervalued. Besides, Lutyens may well have thought he could push him around. Seven years older than him, Baker had always recognised his genius; so much so that he regularly submitted his South African designs to the younger man for his criticism. This Lutyens freely and sometimes caustically supplied. It made Baker's buildings better, and Baker might well have been happy for the relationship to continue on the same lines during their time in Delhi; a fine athlete and sportsman, he was by nature a team player. Alas for their friendship, Lutyens was not a public-school man and did not follow the same rules.

For a short time they were joined by Henry Vaughan Lanchester of Lanchester and Rickards, architects of the flamboyantly Baroque Cardiff City Hall and Law Courts in the centre of Cardiff and of the Methodist Central Hall opposite the Houses of Parliament: 'pale, dark-eyed, and bearded, looking rather like a Spanish grandee of the age of Velasquez'.[3] Again, he was arguably better qualified than Lutyens. But his brilliance was undermined by brusqueness and irritability, and although he returned annually to work on Indian projects until the late 1930s, he did not get government jobs from New Delhi.

North versus South; Eastern versus Western – these simple polarities sum up two major and passionately argued debates. The first relates to the site of the new city. Rising early with a cold bath and cup of tea, the Delhi Town Planning Committee set out to explore the terrain, either by car or elephant. By 9.30am the heat had driven them back to base for another bath and work in the office. In the cool of the evening, they spent a further three hours looking at possible sites, before a third bath and dinner at 8.30pm. As a keen horseman, Baker had the additional advantage of daily rides which took him to all the landmarks left by earlier rulers of Delhi, a city which had been rebuilt again and again – perhaps more than a dozen times. For some time, a northern site was considered. Lord Hardinge believed that he was the person who identified Raisina Hill, to the south, as the final choice – he had been attracted to it from the start. Baker also saw its potential. When building in South

Africa was interrupted by the Boer War, Cecil Rhodes had sent him on a tour of the Mediterranean to study Classical sites. There he had been forcibly impressed by the towering crag of the Acropolis in Athens, the Capitoline Hill in Rome and the 'stupendous platform' of Darius the Great's Persepolis, whose buildings could be seen from all around. He had made use of such a site at Pretoria for the Union Buildings, which were originally to have had a temple behind them: as you approached the complex your appetite would be whetted by the way in which it seemed to disappear, then reappear, according to the rise and fall of the land. To Lutyens, the hill provided the ideal location for a palace that would be the culmination of the whole scheme, agreeing – fatally, as he would later think – that it could be joined by the two Secretariat buildings designed by Baker to house the civil service. Altogether, the plan of New Delhi symbolised, in the words of the Town Planning Committee, the 'peaceful domination and dignified rule over the traditions and life of India by the British Raj'.

The regularity of the plan showed Man to be the master of his surroundings, in the Classical manner, able to bend even Nature to his will. Dominated by straight lines, hexagons and triangles, it is an intellectual tour de force, which perhaps looks better on paper – or from space – than on the ground; as Raymond Unwin could have told him, triangular plots do not combine comfortably with buildings. But for all the geometry, as Jane Ridley describes,

New Delhi is not an orthodox baroque city. The processional route of King's Way is lined not by houses but by trees and open spaces and canals ... the roads are wide and tree-lined, sometimes curving and lined by bungalows set back from the road and surrounded by leafy gardens. The geometry of the hexagons is blurred by leafiness, a juxtaposition of the natural and classical of the kind which Lutyens's gardens had evolved since 1890.[4]

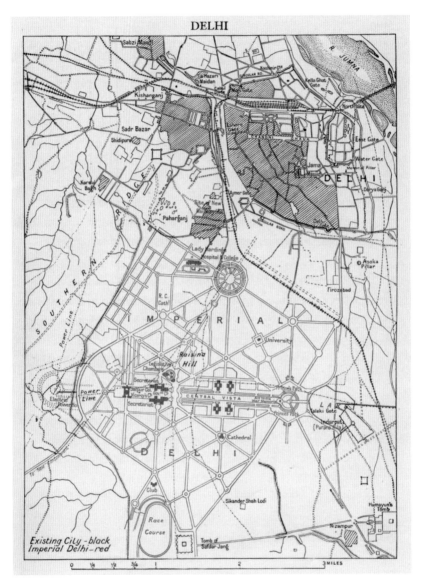

The plan of New Delhi. Avenues are aligned on monuments as in Paris, Rome, Washington and Wren's unexecuted plan for the City of London following the Great Fire. Two overlapping hexagons, themselves divided into smaller geometrical shapes, are preferred to a rectangular grid of streets.

This reflected Lutyens's exposure to Raymond Unwin's radical garden city ideas at Hampstead Garden Suburb and his practical experience of laying out Knebworth Garden Village.

What style of architecture – Eastern or Western – best reflected the ideals of Empire? Lutyens did not go to India with an open mind. He regarded Mughal architecture as 'piffle' before having so much as set foot in the country. Nor was he interested in broadening his horizons. As he wrote:

> Personally I do not believe there is any real Indian architecture or any great tradition. There are just spurts by various mushroom dynasties with as much intellect in them as any other art nouveau.

This was not simply an aesthetic matter: while Kipling, having been partly brought up in India, thrilled to India's colour, cacophony and chaos, Lutyens sought order and could not find it. Architecture, to him, was an index of the collective mind. So he continued:

> There are no doubt great thinkers and good men; but what proof can I find that their thoughts are not as unfinished and as slovenly as the work of that other half of India that offends and distresses the eye at every turn, everywhere, wherever I have been in the Native States or British territory ? There is no trace of any Wren. Is there an Isaac Newton? I doubt it. Without the one you cannot have the other.[5]

Not that Lutyens tried very hard to study the subject and form a more rounded view. According to the Under Secretary of State for India Edwin Montagu:

> He refuses to look at anything about him, he hates Indian architecture as much as ever, he likes straight, final roads and

wants everything levelled … he has absorbed nothing of the country.[6]

He was following in a long-established tradition. 'We ought, like the Romans and the Mohammedans, to take our national style with us,' the architect of the post office and British Hospital in Bombay, T. Roger Smith, had declared.[7] This would set an example and awe Indians by difference. Presumably Lord Curzon had thought so when commissioning the Victoria Memorial in Calcutta, a colossal domed monument of gleaming marble, begun in 1906 – the white elephant of all white elephants. To Lutyens, the geometry of Classicism was eternal, if not divine, and as relevant to the East as the West. When the viceroy, Lord Hardinge attempted to convert him to the beauties of the pointed Indian arch, he replied with the quip: 'Who designed the rainbow?'[8]

There was, however, another view: that, like the Mughal emperors, the Raj should adapt its style to what it found locally. By this method, different ingredients and flavours would be blended into a single eclectic curry – analogous, perhaps, to kedgeree or other Anglo-Indian dishes inspired, but rather different from, Indian originals. By the middle of the 1870s, 'Mussulman', meaning Muslim or, in a term familiarly used at the time, 'Saracenic', had been merged with 'Hindoo', in a decorative coat of many colours that was hung onto the bones of essentially Gothic Revival structure and planning. This was pre-eminently the style of Bombay, expressed *con brio* in the Victoria Terminus of the Great Indian Peninsular Railway, the largest modern building on the subcontinent when it was opened in 1888 after an unprecedented (for India) ten years of building – a work of such bravura that it has proved impervious to its official change of name, being still, to most people, simply VT. Nobody on the Committee admired the recent architecture of Bombay, but Baker took a cultivated interest in Indian architecture and the tide of opinion was moving in his direction.

Posterity has principally learnt of Lutyens's arrogant dismissal of local monuments from his letters to his wife. At first reading, his observations seem typically Edwardian and blinkered: one of several ways in which he was a man of his time. In his defence, we should remember that they were made when Lady Emily was disappearing into the vasty Eastern mists of Theosophy, neglecting her children, not to mention her husband, making Lutyens fear he would lose her completely. While he was on the government payroll as architect of the Viceroy's House, she was also in India, campaigning for the country's independence. His criticisms of Indian architecture could have been part of an attempt to show that not everything about this exotic land was better than home.

The building for which Lutyens was responsible is now called Rashtrapati Bhavan, meaning the Presidential Palace. It is a better name than the Viceroy's House, whose suggestion of domesticity – house rather than palace – belies its character. True, the Viceroy lived there when he had not retreated from the heat of the plains into the hills; but it is no more of a conventional home than Blenheim Palace, a country house built by the government of the day to house a conqueror of the French, the 1st Duke of Marlborough. The Viceroy's House – geometrical, serene, little decorated – contains no memory of the Surrey Hills. Instead it is a monument, built to express the British Empire's sense of itself and (as many saw it) the civilising purpose it had in India. It set Lutyens on course to build other monuments embodying important ideas, such as the Cenotaph and Liverpool Cathedral.

In 1915, with his British practice on hold during the First World War, Lutyens visited neutral Spain, where he designed three palaces for the Duke of Alba and his siblings, although little was realised because of the changed social conditions of the country prior to the

Civil War.[9] This took him to the Escorial, the palace-cum-monastery that the fiercely Roman Catholic and ascetic Philip II had built outside Madrid in the age of the Inquisition. The Escorial is vast and severe – a granite expression of order and self-control, for a king who went to bed in a small room contemplating Hieronymus Bosch's penitential *Seven Deadly Sins and Four Last Things*. Lutyens was impressed; this 'wapping great palace, all very simple and no fraudulent construction as our Government to-day insists on', was one of the few buildings that he said he admired. Majesty was conveyed by large, almost unbroken expanses of wall, rather than ornament. Here is an architecture of massive volumes, articulated by classical forms which have been reduced to their barest, blockiest essentials. While the king himself could walk in rooms decorated with frescoes and lined with books edged with gold, as befitted his station, the overwhelming impression of the Escorial is of austerity – relieved only by a geometrically arranged garden, on a raised platform. Reading John Motley's *The Rise of the Dutch Republic, 1555–66* made Lutyens 'realise the power of which it was the centre'; perhaps the description of the Spanish Empire at its zenith drew a comparison with the British Empire, on which the sun had yet to set. Certainly many of the architectural ideas of the Escorial would be reinterpreted in the Viceroy's House; the great stone staircase flanked by arcades at two levels and the vaulted passages with their patterned floors and multiple pilasters are directly modelled on the Escorial. Everywhere Lutyens's genius lay in seeing that broad effects, in a building of epic scale, were more impressive than a fuss of detail. In this his approach was dramatically different from that of Baker, whose love of symbolism and sympathy for Indian tradition were stronger than his ability to create coherent form.

In the end, Lutyens did adopt some ideas from the monuments he saw in India. He was under pressure to do so, of course; but it also spoke to the gift for synthesising motifs of different origins in a single composition – Little Thakeham, Castle Drogo and the Byzantine-cum-Nedi of Hampstead Garden Suburb are among the many examples. In the Viceroy's House, the civil servants' desire to respect local traditions combined with the demands of the climate almost to compel Lutyens to an entirely new kind of Classicism, with an enormously deep, shadow-giving cornice or *chuja* and a skyline enlivened with *chattris* (temple-like funerary shelters, which he had previously called 'stupid useless things') and fountains that forever flowed (a symbol of abundance in the hot climate). More shade was given by a giant portico and loggias fronted by columns. They are in the Delhi Order, specially designed by Lutyens with decorative bells made of stone so they could never toll the end of a dynasty. As the architectural historian Philip Davies describes it, the stone

Endlessly repeated columns provided a sense of majesty and, in the climate, much-needed shade. They are in the Delhi Order, specially designed by Lutyens with decorative bells made of stone so they could never toll the end of a dynasty.

itself was not only Indian but charged with meaning, being 'the same red sandstone that the Mughals had used at Fatehpur Sikri [the ancient fortified city close to Agra] interspersed with cream stone from Dholpur, Bharatpur and Agra, in brilliant horizontal bands of colour accentuating the horizontal emphasis of the whole edifice'.[10]

Some Indian ideas in fact appealed to him so strongly that he used them on buildings in Britain. There is a mysterious single column on the way to the kitchen at Castle Drogo, for instance, whose form can only be Indian, I would suggest. He often reused the Delhi Order, incorporating hanging bells – not least as the centrepiece of his own rather peculiar coat of arms.

Even the huge copper-clad dome was partly Indian in inspiration. The example of the Great Stupa at Sanchi, in Madhya Pradesh, suggested an improvement on the Western tradition, represented by St Paul's. Partly for structural reasons, great Baroque domes are supported on drums ringed with columns: the profile is stepped and the dome ovoid in shape. While the dome of Bramante's Tempietto at San Pietro in Montorio is hemispherical, it is joined awkwardly to the entablature of the drum. Inspired by the Great Stupa, Lutyens found a more geometrical solution. There is no conventional order around the drum, only closely spaced uprights alternating with bands – a variation of the motif at Sanchi, which seems to imitate weaving. The drum reads as a cylinder; because there is no entablature, the hemispherical dome can rise above it without visual interruption. Lutyens was so struck by the woven stone idea that he used it again in London, for the circular wall enclosing the Philipson Mausoleum in Golders Green Crematorium, as well as the burial enclosure that he made for the Fletcher family on the Rosehaugh estate on the Black Isle, north of Inverness, his most northerly commission;[11] it can also be seen, in simplified form, in the vault over the main staircase in Castle Drogo. As a Buddhist building, the Great Stupa did not speak to many Indians, who were predominantly Hindu or Muslim, but that may have been cleverer that Lutyens knew – no one could accuse the Raj of taking sides in the bitter religious divide.

As in any big government commission, there were constant worries over budget. Costs inevitably ballooned. Lutyens had no sympathy for cheeseparing. 'The Viceroy thinks only of what the place would look like in three years time,' he told Emily. '300 is what I think of.' When he could not get his way with the viceroy, he tried Lady Hardinge. After one spat, he wrote in contrition: 'I shall wash your feet with my tears and dry them with my hair. It is true that I have very little hair but you have very little feet.' But since his bons mots were regarded as official correspondence, they were printed and circulated, to the amusement of junior clerks and no doubt to the chagrin of their author.

At the start of the project, Lord Hardinge sought to emulate the practice of the Mughal emperors and enter his new capital

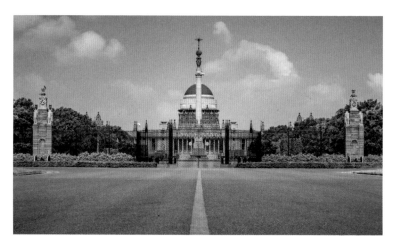

The footprint of the Viceroy's House is bigger than Versailles. Given the vast size, Lutyens used ornament sparingly, instilling calm through long colonnades and bands of coloured stone. Despite reservations, he introduced Indian elements to the Western tradition, expanding the classical vocabulary.

in a ceremonial procession, seated on an elephant. As he did so, a home-made bomb was thrown into the howdah, killing the servant who had been holding his parasol and tearing the flesh of the viceroy's back into strips. Hardinge survived, badly shaken; but the omen was bad. Not perhaps for New Delhi: against heavy odds, the city was built within the lifetimes of its architects and of Hardinge himself. But for Lutyens and Baker, the course of designing it did not run smooth. Famously, a battle over how the two-mile ceremonial King's Way or Rajpath by which the Viceroy's House is approached caused Lutyens – witty through his tears – to meet his 'Bakerloo'. The problem was that, less experienced than his partner in town planning, or tired or inattentive, he had signed off on a survey that showed that the incline of the chosen route included a slight bump. As a result, the Viceroy's House did not stay wholly in the eye of the people journeying towards it – at one point, the bulk of it would disappear below the skyline, leaving only the dome visible. If Baker realised this, he did not warn his friend; perhaps he did not think it mattered. He might have thought that it created a sense of suspense, as he had planned at Pretoria. Besides, it was for Lutyens to undertake the necessary checks and respond accordingly. Once the decision had been made, he found it was impossible to get it altered. Here was not a rich private client who could be charmed or cajoled into spending a bit more money to get a better architectural effect, but a viceroy, a host of committees and a British Government, soon to be engaged in fighting the First World War. Lutyens lobbied everyone he could think of, up to the king. He went on badgering the government to spend the money to level the gradient at a time when, unbeknownst to him, the entire project was in danger of being cancelled on grounds of cost. Baker could have helped him by agreeing to reposition his Secretariat buildings. When he refused to do so, Lutyens made his life hell. As Baker wrote to his wife Florence, he has been too spoilt in always getting his way and he can't now – having come up against something bigger & stronger than he has been accustomed to. I hope it will do him good – and make things easier for me – he is so egotistical – illogical & self willed – that collaboration is a continual difficulty.[12]

Although Baker had a better understanding of topography, and the Acropolis effect of Raisina Hill, its top flattened to provide a platform for the architecture, is essential to the urban drama, Lutyens

The cooling fountains, watercourses and carpet-like geometry of the Mughal Garden, seen here from the top of Viceroy's House, are a far cry from Munstead Wood. One inspiration may have been El Escorial outside Madrid. Taken in 2005, this photograph shows the dense planting of trees beyond the garden, reminiscent of the Garden City ideal.

was unquestionably the greater architect. But greatness cannot excuse the petulance of his behaviour.

For most of the ensuing century, history took Lutyens's side. With his flair for publicity, he ensured that the loser of Bakerloo would get his account set down in print. His tool for doing so was Robert Byron, a brilliant young travel writer who, on the official opening in 1931, was chosen to describe New Delhi both in *Country Life* and the *Architectural Review*. Aged only twenty-six, he was unable to resist Lutyens's genius and charm. The articles praised Lutyens to the skies and slated Baker. It was a mean trick on Lutyens's part. He crowed when he saw the magazines in print.

This does not show Lutyens in an attractive light but he was always a driven man. Great artists will stop at nothing to have their ideas realised. New Delhi was laid out, the Viceroy's House was built; extraordinary resources had to be mobilised, hundreds of thousands of workers employed and many nay-sayers to be overcome for this to be accomplished. Only strong and single-minded people could have made it happen. The result has been called an 'architecture of power', and people's responses to it often depend on their view of the British Empire.

This can overlook the aesthetic brilliance of the achievement, recognised by the successive Indian governments since Independence who have treated the Rashtrapati Bhavan and other monuments with exemplary care. Ultimately, New Delhi is an irony: it exemplifies the unification of British India, bound together by the railways. Without the railways, the campaign for independence could not have grown into a pan-Indian movement. Completed in 1931, it was also an emblem of a different era, that of the Motor Durbar of 1911. In the intervening years four empires – Russian, German, Austro-Hungarian and Ottoman – had fallen, and it could only be a matter of time before Britain's own empire, the mightiest of all, would dissolve. The map of the world had been redrawn by the Great War.

TEN

KNOWN UNTO GOD

The Stone of Remembrance (War Stone) 1917
Temporary Cenotaph at Whitehall 1919. Rebuilt in stone 1920
Thiepval Memorial to the Missing 1923–30

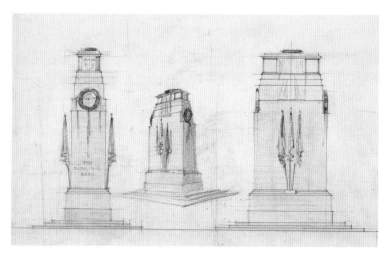

Early sketch for the Cenotaph dated 'June 4th, 1919'. Originally a temporary structure which returning soldiers could salute to remember their fallen comrades in a Peace Parade, it proved so popular with the public that it was erected in Portland stone the next year.

HARDLY A FAMILY IN THE LAND WAS UNTOUCHED by the Great War. More than one in twenty of Britain's adult male population was killed – eight hundred and eighty thousand troops. For decades, what the French called *mutilés de guerre* would be a familiar sight on the nation's streets. On top of the appalling human sacrifice on the Front was the upheaval to life at home. Architects were among the professional groups who found that work had dried up: Lutyens, always anxious about money, wondered if his savings would see him through the crisis. It was a national trauma that stirred a welter of profound emotions – loss, grief, fear, incomprehension, hope, despair and rage. In a land where the outward display of feeling was often suppressed, people turned spontaneously to folk symbols to articulate their anguish. Wayside shrines appeared as crossroads. As early as 1915, three years before the Armistice, the discussion about the best way to remember the Fallen was underway.

This would lead to a movement to build war memorials, which generally named all the young men from the area who had lost their lives. There was a need for national monuments, civic monuments, war cemeteries, regimental memorials, smaller memorials erected by village committees, as well as schools, colleges, workplaces, railway companies, religious bodies, trades unions, Inns of Court, the United Grand Lodge of Freemasons, the Royal Horticultural Society and even bicyclists. It is thought that a hundred thousand war memorials were constructed in the years following 1918. Except for the regimental memorials, they were a previously unknown building type. Before the First World War, almost no memorials had been erected to remember the common soldiers and sailors who died in war. The Duke of Wellington famously regarded his infantry as scum (although he took unusual trouble to preserve them on the battlefield, as a valuable resource). Only officers had tablets or statues erected to them in churches and cathedrals. The rank and file were hastily thrown into mass graves, packed with lime to speed decomposition. Sensibilities began to change in the Victorian period. A Crimean War memorial in Cheltenham, unveiled in 1858, takes the form of a large black cast-iron plinth which used to support a canon captured at Sebastopol, until it was melted down for munitions in the Second World War: a plaque lists all the Fallen soldiers from the borough. Memorials with a scope of this kind are rare in the Victorian period. By the time of the Boer War, other ranks were being named as well as officers and occasionally a statue of a private would march onto the top of the memorial to be given pride of place – but they were soldiers of the regiment rather than local boys. That war had been fought by a small professional army. By 1918 the British army comprised three million, eight hundred thousand men, supported by three million soldiers and labourers from across the Empire. Here was warfare on a previously unimagined scale – and one reason to build memorials was the hope that remembering the horror would stop it happening again. With no precedent to follow, the memorials that remembered the dead – along with the ceremonies that went with them – had to be invented afresh: sometimes hastily, to meet the needs of the moment. Lutyens was in the thick of the discussions and his contribution can seem all-pervasive. Not only did he design the Cenotaph on Whitehall, the War Stone that was placed in all the larger war cemeteries on the Front, the Thiepval Arch to the missing of the Battle of the Somme, and over a hundred war cemeteries in France and Belgium, but he helped shape the vision that the war cemeteries expressed. Beyond that, he designed scores of naval, military, civic, local and family memorials across Britain. At a practical level, the work kept his practice going. More profoundly, it gave him the opportunity to develop the great symbolic language that he would deploy in all his subsequent major projects. His conception of it was entirely different from the more conventional imagery favoured by other architects and the Church of England, but instantly resonated with the British public and, a century later, remains just as powerful today.

Now in his mid forties, Lutyens was too old to serve in the war. Of course, like so many people, he was certainly touched by it, and five of his nephews were killed. And yet, despite the collapse of his practice at home, he was better off than other architects, particularly those who had previously designed country houses: he could go either to neutral Spain – where he had several big commissions from grandees – or India, where work continued on New Delhi. But building projects were dogged by problems. In the summer of 1915 he dashed to Rome, where the British School had got hopelessly bogged down. This was partly because Lutyens's office had failed to supply drawings, partly because the clerk of works was (according to Lutyens) 'quite stupid and useless', and no longer on speaking terms with the builder's representative, who was himself hampered from interpreting local byelaws, regulations and customs by not speaking Italian. On top of everything was the disruption caused by the war, given that materials had to be sent out from Britain. A consignment of cast-iron pipes went down when the SS *Bittern* was torpedoed.[1] Otherwise, for the first two years of the war he was as detached as anyone could be from the conflict.

But on returning from India in the summer of 1917, he was invited to advise the Imperial War Graves Commission on the shape of war cemeteries in France. 'What humanity can endure, suffer, is beyond belief,' he exclaimed to Emily on a visit of inspection.

> The grave-yards, haphazard from the needs of much to do and little time for thought – and then a ribbon of isolated graves like a milky way across miles of country, where men were tucked in where they fell – Ribbons of little crosses each touching each across a cemetery – set in a wilderness of annuals, – and where one sort of flower has grown the effect is charming, easy, and oh so pathetic, that one thinks no other monument is needed.

Other symbols would be needed, however – indeed, he lit upon two of them when describing 'the poppies and wildflowers – that are as friendly to an unexploded shell as they are to the leg of a garden seat in Surrey'. Poppies would become an enduring emblem of remembrance after the British Legion began to sell artificial ones in 1921. Flowers chosen by Gertrude Jekyll would become a feature of the war cemeteries when they were built. Architecturally Lutyens could suggest no form beyond a perfect sphere. As he wrote, words muddling themselves in the stress of the emotion he clearly felt:

> The only monument can be one where the endeavour is sincere to make such a monument permanent – a solid ball of bronze!

At the time of the French Revolution, the architect Étienne-Louis Boullée had proposed an architecture of spheres and cones, megalomaniac in size, little of which was built; it seems unlikely that Lutyens would have known of it. But his idea has a similarly visionary if not messianic quality. Had his imagination turned to the flaming gilded orb on top of the Monument in the City of

London? The ball of bronze was never made but Lutyens did not abandon the principle that only geometry could express the weight of meaning that such a monument would have to bear.

In early July 1919, Lutyens was summoned by the prime minister, David Lloyd George. The government needed a 'catafalque' in Whitehall where the great procession of Allied leaders and military units was due to take place as part of the Peace Celebrations later that month, following the conclusion of the Treaty of Versailles. Not a catafalque, Lutyens replied, 'but a Cenotaph'. His mind had gone back to an afternoon in the garden of Munstead Wood when someone had likened a large bench to the Cenotaph of Sigismunda. In the Classical world, a cenotaph was an empty tomb erected to a dead person buried elsewhere: the Cenotaph in Whitehall – the first version of which was erected in wood and plaster to imitate stone – is a plinth waiting for a coffin that will never come, because the Fallen lie overseas. Lutyens sketched the main lines of the monument in a letter to Lady Sackville the same day and they never changed. (Though there may be an element of myth-making here: he could have been given prior warning of the prime minister's request. A drawing for the Cenotaph dated June 4, 1919 exists in the Imperial War Museum.[2]) The Cenotaph made no appeal to religious feeling. To Lutyens this was important. Among the hundreds of thousands of men who had died were many who were not Christians; they might, like the Indian regiments, have followed other faiths, or none. The only decoration was a wreath, rendered apparently in stone, the only words: TO THE GLORIOUS DEAD. Although obscure in meaning, austere in form and all but devoid of conventional symbols, it was immediately understood by the public – 'people of every sort and condition lined from dawn till dark to lay their pathetic tributes before it,' wrote Christopher Hussey. *The Times* led the call for it to be made permanent.

Simple, grave and beautiful in design, it has been universally recognised as a just and fitting memorial of those who have made the greatest sacrifice; and the flowers which have been daily laid upon it since the march show the strength of its appeal to the imagination.

On Armistice Day – November 11 – the next year, a replacement made of white Portland stone was unveiled.

This Cenotaph was not precisely the same as its predecessor. Lutyens had made it an object of great geometrical refinement, based on the ancient Greek concept of entasis, or optical adjustment. To Lutyens, 'the Parthenon in Athens eclipses everything else created by man,' although he made the mistake of attributing the maths to Archimedes who lived over two centuries after it was built.[3]

… Bear in mind that all the vertical lines tend to converge upwards to a specific point and that all the horizontals represent surfaces of spheres described from another specific point below.

His calculations for the Cenotaph covered thirty-three pages of his notebook; they were elaborate, precise and – given that most of the public who paid their respects at the Cenotaph cannot have noticed them – arcane. In a letter to Sir Alfred Mond, when he sent him the revised designs, Lutyens wrote:

I have made slight alterations to meet the conditions demanded by the setting out of its lines on subtle curvatures, the difference is almost imperceptible, yet sufficient to give it a sculpturesque quality and a life, that cannot pertain to rectangular blocks of stone.[4]

All the surfaces curve almost imperceptibly so that the verticals would meet at a point one thousand feet above the ground, and the horizontals nine hundred feet to the side. Templates were cut to make them. Where Lutyens acquired his knowledge of mathematics – given that he had barely been to school – is unknown. Perhaps it was one of the few useful legacies of his unfortunate father, Charles Lutyens: there must have been a mathematical component to the rangefinder he invented. Ned's daughter Mary thought he might have picked up something from his elder brother Fred, who went to Westminster School and Trinity College, Cambridge. Today, the effects of a century of weather have made the entasis difficult

The Cenotaph in Whitehall, focus of Britain's ceremonies of remembrance since the First World War. Remarkably, it is an almost entirely abstract structure, devoid of religious symbolism but built according to elaborate mathematical calculations.

to see; but the Cenotaph remains the natural and unchallenged focus of the observances that take place on November 11 each year.

For the war cemeteries in France, Lutyens joined Herbert Baker and Reginald Blomfield on a working party to establish how architecture would meet the unprecedented challenge. Nine hundred war cemeteries are scattered in an irregular line between France's border with Switzerland and the North Sea, in an extraordinary national endeavour to give respect and dignity to the dead. It was decided at an early stage in the war that no family would be able to repatriate the body of a fallen soldier, whatever his rank: all would be buried where they died. The principle of equality in death would be extended to the headstones that marked the graves. All would be made of white limestone, all to the same shape and dimensions: one foot three inches broad, three inches thick, the top forming a segment of a circle two feet six inches in diameter. The curve of the top would throw off rain, reducing the wear to the inscriptions. The latter were largely restricted to the name, age and military rank of the soldier, with his regimental badge at the top. The body of every soldier who could be recovered was given a headstone. Headstones of soldiers whose remains could not be identified bore the words A British Soldier Known Unto God. They stand beside each other in lines as disciplined as a parade ground, by their dozens or by their hundreds, with familiar flowers nestling at their feet. Today, a century on, the last of the generation to fight in the First World War is long dead and direct connection with it is broken; nevertheless, the British and Commonwealth war cemeteries – so many of them, so well cared for, so dignified – reduce many people to speechlessness or tears. The aesthetic is different from the black crosses and ossuaries of the French war cemeteries or the forest gloom of the few German ones; so is the emphasis on the individual. I do not know how credit for the ideas should be apportioned because it is impossible to follow the discussions of the working party, but they are consonant with the humanism to which Lutyens subscribed.

The principles are Classical. Classicism had become the architecture of Empire and of great civic projects through the bombastic medium of Imperial Baroque. As suited their sombre purpose, the style of the war cemeteries is more restrained. Permanence was a criterion from the start; even if the architecture of the war cemeteries fell into decay it would still survive as ruins. It is not obvious now but the construction of the cemeteries was a huge feat of engineering, with levelling needed for order and drainage to prevent flooding. Classicism provided a repertoire of forms. It enabled the spaces of the cemeteries to be organised with quiet seemliness. The different classical elements of colonnades, balustrades, arches and obelisks gain in meaning through repetition. There is an air of understatement which makes the emotional impact of row upon row of headstones all the greater. While the attempt was made to make all the graves face east, the direction from which the enemy had come, there is little that is overtly jingoistic.

It was decided that there should also be symbolic elements to provide a focus in each cemetery. To Baker and Blomfield, the natural form for such memorial architecture was the cross. As well as its obvious religious significance, it stood for suffering and oblation. Blomfield designed a Cross of Sacrifice which incorporated an inverted bronze sword, inspired by one hanging on the wall of his home in Kent. On an octagonal base, this would be placed in every war cemetery with over forty graves. The cross idea was supported by Charles Aike, the director of the Tate Gallery who was another member of the commission, and leaders of the churches. Across Britain, many of the thousands of committees responsible for erecting memorials in towns and villages voted to have a cross of some kind: it became the most popular form. This did not however speak to Lutyens. His wife's Theosophy had made him all too aware that not everyone subscribed to the established Church of England with George V as its head. Muslims, Hindus, Jews and atheists had also given their lives. He proposed a mighty slab of limestone, twelve feet in length: it would be like an altar, evoking the sacrifice of the men buried beneath the serried ranks of white headstones before it. Altars had been used by all the ancient religions. Standing on a plinth formed of three steps – 'the upper and lower steps of a width twice that of the centre step to give due dignity' – it would face west, facing the graves of the soldiers. The surfaces of the stone would be modelled with preternatural subtlety, the horizontals being segments of vast spheres 1,801ft 8ins in diameter. Naturally, as Lutyens wrote, 'the greatest possible amount of labour and thought [were] required in its manufacture' – which seems to have added to its almost occult significance.[5] Here was the ball motif on a giant scale. To most people, the slight curvature would have been barely apparent, if not impossible to detect; but God – as Lutyens liked to say on other occasions – would have seen. In the end, it was decided against calling it an altar: Lutyens's friend J.M. Barrie said that sounded too 'churchy' and would offend the Scots. Instead Lutyens jotted down a 'stoneology' of possible other names – The Stone. The War Stone. The Great War Stone. The White Stone. The King Emperor's Stone, The Stone of Reverence. The Stone of Britain. The Battle Stone. The Stone of Peace … By default it became known as the War Stone (although at a later point this came to seem too militaristic and the Stone of Remembrance is now generally used). The low lines suited the landscape of Picardy and the Pas-de-Calais, unlike the crosses of Baker and Blomfield. 'I think there is something rather grand in its simplicity about this proposal,' Barrie told the director of the War Graves Commission, General Fabian Ware. '… Lutyens's is one of the most imaginative minds I have ever known.' The War Stone was placed in all the larger cemeteries.

Altogether Lutyens was responsible for one hundred and twenty-seven cemeteries – fifteen per cent of the total. It had been decided to use a stable of architects to avoid sameness, and the scale of the undertaking was such that Lutyens himself had to preside over a team of talented assistants, whose ideas (unusually) he sometimes accepted. The work could be Florentine (Béthune Town Cemetery) or Cotswolds (Adelaide Cemetery, where the pavilions have rough walls with a sunburst of tile over the arch); bunker-like (Klein-Vierstraat British Cemetery) or soaring (Villers-Bretonneux Military Cemetery and Australian Memorial to the Missing). Common to many of them is a repertoire of inventive

Étaples Military Cemetery in the Pas-de-Calais, showing Lutyens's 'great altar stone' (or Stone of Remembrance) conceived as a symbol of common sacrifice after a visit to battlefield cemeteries in 1917. The subtle geometry made it expensive to carve, so it was reserved for cemeteries of more than a thousand graves. The concrete crosses here mark French graves.

themes and approaches which provide a new emotional language. They include the frozen drapery of Étaples, an enormous cemetery created for the soldiers who died at the big hospital there: Lutyens preferred flags carved out of stone to ordinary flags, whose flapping would have disturbed the Zen-like repose of the architecture; he had begun to develop the idea at the Theosophical Society Building where drops, apparently of fabric bound with ribbon, are realised in a heavy manner and set either side of a fireplace. Wreaths and garlands are rendered in similarly monumental style.

We see a simpler yet more demonstrative idiom emerging. Classical forms are, partly on grounds of cost, pared back to their bare essentials, but then assembled in more complex ways. An example is the entrance building at Serre Road Cemetery No. 2. Lutyens began to use an elemental language, in which ornament – stripped of carving – is reduced to basic geometrical forms such as discs and squares. This first appears in the India Gate at New Delhi (it is difficult not to notice the similarity with contemporary Art Deco in France). Lutyens was experienced in the design of gardens but the war cemeteries required a broader approach. Their boldly geometrical layout is reminiscent of Beaux-Arts planning – or more directly, that of New Delhi.

The supreme masterpiece of the new approach is the Memorial to the Missing of the Somme at Thiepval. This commemorates a grim fact of war: after five and a half months of heavy bombardment, in the second half of 1916, during which small pieces of land were fought over and changed hands many times, the bodies of seventy-two thousand British and South African troops were never recovered. Some hastily dug battlefield cemeteries were pounded during subsequent action; of the men buried nothing identifiable could be found. It fell to Lutyens to design their memorial. He did so in a spirit that was quite different from that of the War Stone, whose low profile and delicately carved pale limestone complemented the chalk downland of Northern France. This monument would be a huge arch, placed on the brow of a hill. It would be made largely of red brick. Built in 1928–32, it reared above a landscape still bald of trees after the fighting. Even today, it can be seen from miles away, its head lifted menacingly above a clump of trees. The structure is alien to the rolling fields that surround it, out of scale, a crescendo of straight lines and rectangles – a cry of … what? Anguish and anger, possibly. Rage against the brutality that had deprived so many young men of all trace of their earthly existence. These are personal reflections on my part. What can surely be said is that the Thiepval Arch is not a beautiful object. It would be a worse piece of architecture if it were.

Thiepval had been Lutyens's first choice of site. It was on the brow of the slope and the hottest point of the whole front, due to the presence of an old quarry; the Germans had developed

The Thiepval Memorial to the Missing remembers soldiers whose bodies were never recovered from the Somme. Panels on the walls of this elaborate triumphal arch are carved with the names of the Fallen.

this into the Leipzig Redoubt. For reasons of economy, the government initially insisted a different location, on high ground at St Quentin, where at one point Lutyens proposed that his arch should straddle a road. The St Quentin scheme was abandoned as part of a reassessment of the number of free-standing memorials proposed for the Somme, and the Thiepval monument agreed as part of an Anglo-French commemoration, recognising the joint nature of operations. Lutyens reused his St Quentin design which had been approved 'with acclamation' by the Imperial War Graves Commission at the end of December 1924 and exhibited at the Royal Academy the next year. Essentially it is a variant of one of the most enduring motifs in Classical architecture, the triumphal arch. Triumphal arches were erected by victorious generals in Ancient Rome: they consisted of a tall central arch with two smaller ones, flanked by columns or pilasters, the whole composition enriched by carved trophies and capped by an attic storey bearing inscriptions. Napoleon copied the idea for his Arc de Triomphe in Paris. As Peter Howell describes in *The Triumphal Arch*, numerous architects reinterpreted the motif, whether as eyecatchers in landscape parks or applied decoratively, for example to the façades of buildings such as Kedleston Hall, in Derbyshire. Lutyens himself used the motif in his Rand Regiments Memorial, now called the Anglo-Boer War Memorial, at Saxonwold in South Africa, first proposed in 1904 although not completed with the installation of the giant Angel of Peace which crowns its dome until 1914. At Thiepval, however, he does something unprecedented. He takes the structural essence of the idea, strips it of all extraneous ornament and reimagines it in three dimensions. Most Roman triumphal arches were not elaborately volumetric: they acted as gateways through which a triumphal procession might pass. Occasionally a cross arch was added at ninety degrees to the main façade. Lutyens's great arch, however, is interpenetrated by numerous cross arches. Far from resembling the simple, flat and richly ornamented structures of the ancient world, it is an essay in pure form, whose complex geometry speaks for itself, with minimal decoration of any kind. The arch dominates its hill top. Even today, now that trees have grown up around it, the upper section can be seen for miles around. To achieve the necessary height, Lutyens made the central arch much taller than the subordinate ones around its skirts – another departure from Classical precedent. Altogether it is as though an ancient theme in music has been turned by the greatest of composers into an elaborate fugue. The inspiration was the need for large expanses of wall surfaces on which to apply limestone panels. Whereas the Cenotaph in London provided an abstract focus for the nation's grief, the Thiepval Arch expressed the government's determination that each soldier who died should be remembered as an individual. As we have seen, the remains of every British soldier that was recovered received an individual burial, beneath a white headstone in a military cemetery, even though his identity was unknown. But the Missing whose bodies were never recovered could not be buried; instead the name, rank and regiment of each one of them was carved in Roman lettering onto the sides of the arch.

In the introduction to the third of the *Memorial Volumes* published after Lutyens's death, the architect A.S.G. Butler describes the Thiepval Arch as 'a solid geometrical composition of arches and their supports, more advanced than anything Lutyens had previously done towards completed abstraction' – and almost too difficult to describe in words. Gavin Stamp, in *The Memorial to the Missing of the Somme*, likens its step-like massing to the pyramids of Egypt and other monuments of the ancient world that were then attracting the attention of European architects. I find another contemporary resonance, with Futurist works such as Umberto Boccioni's *Unique Forms of Continuity in Space* of 1931.

The Futurists were enthralled by the speed and aggression of the Machine Age. Lutyens was appalled by its inhumanity; his Thiepval Arch expresses not movement but the opposite – immovable mass. And yet it is (to me) ugly in the way that his age was ugly: the age that had inflicted on the youth of Europe the cataclysmic violence of the Great War.

ELEVEN

I DON'T KNOW WHAT YOU MEAN BY 'ABOUT'

36 Smith Square 1912

Queen Mary's Dolls' House 1921

Midland Bank, 196a Piccadilly 1922

Midland Bank HQ, 27–32 Poultry 1924–39

Park House (Mells), Somerset 1925

Midland Bank, 140 Leadenhall Street 1928

Midland Bank, King Street Manchester 1929–32

Halnaker House, West Sussex 1930

The motif that Lutyens designed for the top of the dome of the Midland Bank head office in Poultry, City of London. A hand is raised in pontifical blessing, but with a coin held in its palm. The idea was rejected.

T HE CHANCELLOR OF THE EXCHEQUER FOR MOST
of 1915 had been Reginald McKenna. A devout
Congregationalist, he could be acerbic in the House of
Commons but he was, for a politician, a modest man, with no desire
to see his name perpetuated after his term in office had been served.
Consequently, he is not widely remembered among the statesmen of
the First World War. But his friend, the economist John Maynard
Keynes left a warm portrait:

> Reggie McKenna was at his best in his own deeply loved
> family circle. His wife had inherited from her mother, Lady
> Jekyll, the fairest traditions not of the great but of the middle
> houses of England where the hostess's personal attention
> to the happiness of her guests raised bodily comfort above
> itself to become the gentlest of the muses. In leisured talk,
> in the setting of music and of country sights and smells, one
> at least kept the Sabbath, even in time of war, by abstaining
> from work.

Marrying late, 'he who had been too long a bachelor learnt the tenderness of life'. McKenna became one of the greatest of Lutyens's clients, who helped plug the gap left by the dearth of country-house commissions after the conflict. In 1919 he became Chairman of the Midland Bank.

Six years older than Lutyens, his early years had been similarly impecunious. Following a bank failure in 1866, his father split the family, sending the youngest members, including Reggie, to live cheaply in France and Germany with their mother. The stay would stand him in good stead. Senior Liberal MPs were not conspicuous for their mastery of languages. To quote Lord Claud Hamilton, a Unionist MP:

> Balfour knew no French; Lord Grey speaks French disgraceful on the lips of a Foreign Secretary; Mr Asquith's French is excessively bad; Mr Runciman speaks fair French, and Mr McKenna speaks fluent conversational though not colloquial French – but then McKenna never went to any of our great public schools.[1]

Academically, the school that McKenna attended – King's College School, then part of King's College in the Strand – was better than most but it was not Eton or Harrow: a difference of which he was conscious in the Cabinet. At Cambridge, where he got in on a scholarship, he was a rowing blue. Afterwards he became a barrister, although always with a self-doubting eye on politics. 'What assurance have I that I shall ever have the opportunity to use this politically much instructed but inferior wit of mine?' he wrote in his diary. 'At four and twenty, without a penny, I study Burke to learn the art of statesmanship. Ye Gods, what assurance!'[2] It was the support of his brothers Ernest and Theodore that enabled him to become the MP for North Monmouthshire in 1895. Eleven years later he was sufficiently established to become the subject of a Spy cartoon in *Vanity Fair*. 'He is popular with his own side, and behind his air of aggression is earnest and sensitive.'[3]

When H.H. Asquith became prime minister in 1908, McKenna was made First Lord of the Admiralty. That year he married Pamela, the younger of Sir Herbert Jekyll's two daughters, twenty-six years his junior; clever and musical, she became a friend of the composer Sir Hubert Parry, director of the Royal College of Music, as well as being enrolled by Asquith in the 'harem' of young woman friends with whom he liked to flirt. (It was not a match that delighted the family, who were 'all rather skiffy coffy' over it, as Lutyens told Emily.) Marriage, in Lutyens's book, meant building a home; but the McKennas were already provided with one, having an official residence at the Admiralty. In *Lutyens and the Edwardians*, Jane Brown suggests that McKenna could well have consoled Ned by introducing him to his Cambridge friend Dr Bond, for whom Lutyens built Middlefield – one of his most disciplined small country-house compositions, dominated by a deep roof and three tall chimneys. Two years later, McKenna swapped Cabinet jobs with Winston Churchill, becoming home secretary: it was time to build and build quickly. His wife Pamela and 'the whole Jekyll family' were pro-Lutyens. If McKenna felt he had been caught, he was not to regret it. 'The whole Jekyll family', extending beyond the Jekyll fastness of Munstead to Mells Manor, in Somerset, where Sir Herbert's sister-in-law Frances was chatelaine, provided the domestic security that he had lacked as a child. They played the same role for Lutyens. Soon, Lutyens's letters were opening 'My dear McReggie' – a foretaste of the MacSack and MacNed with which the exotic, luxury-loving Lady Sackville and he would address each other in their strangely infantilising amour beginning later in the decade.

McKenna had strong views about architecture, as presumably did his brother Theo, a solicitor whose hobby was 'designing country houses, of which he made beautiful models', according to his obituary in *The Times*.[4] Reggie would draw out plans on squared paper before Lutyens got to work. It is unclear how much Reggie influenced the plan for 36 Smith Square, a short walk from the Houses of Parliament, but certainly the house expressed his personality. It was 'so like him,' remembered Ernest Raymond in *Uncensored Celebrities*.

> It is solid, efficient, advantageously placed, built of the very best pressed bricks, irreproachably British, and a little forbidding in its aggressive freshness … go inside and you will find every evidence of taste and education: … there will be the due touch of old culture to correct the oiled smoothness of modern convenience: and yet – well, if you happen to be fanciful you will feel the grit just as you did out … For grit, in both senses, enters into the very being of Mr Reginald McKenna.[5]

The site occupies a corner with Dean Trench Street. Lutyens made the entrance on the narrower façade, on Smith Square. Arriving guests found themselves in a low, vaulted hall: the staircase was only seen when they had turned a corner at the end. 'McKenna thinks my staircase is a miracle,' Lutyens reported to Emily (alas, it was replaced by the next owners). Here they climbed to the enfilade of dining room, library and drawing room on the piano nobile along Dean Trench Street, with the drawing room occupying the whole width of the Smith Square front as well. 'I have just been given the whole of the panelling and carving of an immense Georgian room which will look perfect in our new dining room', Pamela told the Admiralty civil servant Vincent Baddeley. 'I am *too* lucky!"

The early Georgian style of the exterior was a given. Although at first glance the terraces of Smith Square appear to be contemporary with Thomas Archer's central St John's church, built in 1713–28, three of the sides are really a creation of the early twentieth century, made possible, in the case of number 36, by the sinking of deep piles through the soft ground to reach a sound bottom. Facetiously (since he lived some streets away), Pamela hoped that Baddeley had not been 'inconvenienced like most of the other inhabitants of Westminster by our building operations. We have had furious letters from Mr Stead, Capt Anson and several lawyers saying that their glass and crockery had all been shattered by the violent shocks produced by the pile-driving.'[6]

Lutyens loved the McKennas and they would become important clients after the First World War; for the time being, however, their architectural ambitions had been fulfilled (McKenna was not, at this stage of his career, a rich man). But in Somerset, Pamela's aunt Frances Horner lived at Mells Manor; she was another of Lutyens's friends and a champion of his work. There Lutyens had begun to help Frances and her husband Sir John turn the Manor and its village into a work of art.

The Horner family had owned Mells since the Dissolution of the Monasteries. In the early eighteenth century, they had left the manor house and built a house in their landscaped park: Park House was light, regular and set away from the village. But like other landowning families at the turn of the twentieth century, John and Frances Horner were forced to economise. They went back to the manor house – somewhat reluctantly, although manor houses had returned to aesthetic favour, in an age that valued old craftsmanship and romance over light rooms and rational plans. During the Victorian era, many such ancient homes, like Tess's home in Thomas Hardy's novel, had fallen down the social scale to become farmhouses or cottages, or were simply left to collapse; there were many of them in the West Country. Mells Manor had fared better. It was converted into an Anglican college for the training of craftsmen, some of whose stained glass can be seen in the church. Even so, part of the house was in ruins by 1900 when the Horners returned to it.

As a girl, Frances had worn autumn leaves in her hair and Liberty velveteen in soft shades; she was the daughter of the port merchant William Graham, a major collector of early Renaissance and pre-Raphaelite pictures. While a younger sister became a missionary in China, Frances lived for art. Edward Burne-Jones developed a passion for her and was devastated when she went 'and married a market gardener' (in other words, bumpkin) at Mells. One of The Souls, she was said to have 'ghost eyes'.[7] Resisting the handsome Detmar Blow, practically house architect to The Souls and a practised hand at romantic manor houses, she and John commissioned Lutyens. Frances became one of his firmest friends and, as she recalled in *Time Remembered*, he 'beautified every house I had anything to do with'.[8] Money was tight: it did not run to implementing the full-blown scheme for the manor house which Lutyens designed in 1904. Nevertheless, the whole medieval complex at Mells – manor house, church and village – became aesthetically perfect. The manor house provided the ideal setting for antiquarian objects, such as the veil worn by Mary, Queen of Scots at her execution, which the Roman Catholic Horner family had collected over the centuries. The important library was installed in panelling designed and partly made by Herbert Jekyll, who had a passion for wood carving. After the First World War, Lutyens added a music room to the manor house to contain the 'Orpheus' piano painted for Frances by Burne-Jones.

In 1908 Lutyens had the sad task of designing a memorial shelter above the stream to remember the Horners' son Mark who had died at the age of sixteen. In Mark's memory his parents gave a new water supply to the village. Lutyens's structure is triangular, placed so that the stream becomes a living metaphor – the river of life. The lettering was carved by Eric Gill. Nine years later Fate struck a double blow when Park House burnt down in October 1917 and the Horners' only surviving son Edward, an officer in the 18th Hussars, died in the Battle of Cambrai the next month. His memorial is one of Lutyens's most romantic and poignant conceptions. On top of a plinth stands a statue by Alfred Munnings, the greatest equestrian artist of his day, showing Horner on horseback: the image of a latter-day knight. A letter scribbled to Lady Horner dated July 9, 1918 has found its way into the McKenna papers in the Churchill Archives Centre in Cambridge, in which Lutyens describes the idea. Since it has not been published before I quote it in full.

A present day uniform would be better [presumably than armour] but more difficult to achieve wh. makes an attempt more worth while. Do cavalry wear tin hats? Could you get a photo of a man in the 18th Hussars in 1914 war kit?

I think the statue would look best – not to walk round – as the chapel cannot be large. Yet far enough out to show well through the existing North window. We might get real flags to hang.

But I am not sure of flags behind the statue (as a trophy?)

A horse with legs au clair [clearly visible?] will need to be in bronze? unless there is a post under him.

Well I will make a sketch & then you (all [?]) can discuss it & we can make more and more!

This is accompanied by two doodles showing mounted horsemen wearing broad-brimmed helmets; in the end, it was wisely decided for Edward to be sculpted bare-headed, with his helmet attached to his saddle. A proposed extension to the church in which the memorial would have been surrounded by columns was abandoned in favour of placing it in the centre of the Horner Chapel. It has since been moved to a more prominent position.

At the back of the church, carved by Eric Gill directly into the stone of the wall, is a Latin inscription with a bronze wreath hanging above it. It remembers Horner's brother-in-law Raymond Asquith, who had been an outstanding Classical scholar; 'so gifted and yet so devoid of personal ambition,' wrote Winston Churchill to his grieving father, the prime minister H.H. Asquith. Together, the memorials symbolise the twin lodestars by which the British officers educated at the public schools steered their lives: Christian chivalry and the Classics.

In 1919 the architect returned to Mells, trudging around the village with a committee to select a site for the village war memorial. He designed a tall Tuscan column with a figure of St George slaying the dragon on top. It rises above a curved wall with benches for the laying of wreaths. The inscription concludes: 'THIS STONE IS RAISED TO US IN THE HOME OF OUR DELIGHT'. The McKennas' children were too young to fight in the war but the family would know its own tragedy when one of their sons, Michael, died at the age of twenty-one in 1932 from septicemia after a minor operation in hospital. Lutyens designed a three-dimension grave slab, incorporating stylised crosses. By then – as we shall see – McKenna was providing the mainstay to his practice.

Mells illustrates the change that had come over Lutyens's world. With hindsight we can see that Lutyens's country-house practice had run its course: his genius needed the bigger canvas of great public commissions such as New Delhi and Liverpool Cathedral to work on. In this respect, the War served him well, since it provided numerous opportunities for monumental architecture, including the Cenotaph, the war cemeteries and the Thiepval Arch. That was not, of course, how it seemed at the time. While Lutyens was lucky to have work, country houses had provided his bread and butter. He was not as badly off as Voysey or Blow; when Lutyens ran into Blow, he found that he had nothing on hand beyond his own house in the Cotswolds and was working as a factotum for the Duke of Westminster – a relationship that would end in disaster. Where projects were commissioned from Lutyens – an addition to Muncaster Castle in Cumberland costing £100,000, a memorial church and village in Essex for the sportsman and millionaire Major James Morrison DSO – they mostly ran into the sands. 'Morrison says bring laundry down if you like to stay,' Ned wrote to his wife, in a sign of the times. '… Rural conditions difficult.' In addition to which, building materials were rationed and young craftsmen were either dead or displaced.

Besides, architecture itself was changing. The national effort had also hastened innovation: factories and workers' housing were run up quickly using prefabricated elements; the Nissen hut, invented by an officer of the Royal Engineers in 1916, was on its way. All Europe had pivoted towards the use of industrial processes which were at the opposite remove to the solid, handmade architecture of the Arts and Crafts Movement. There was also a social revolution. Servants who had gone to work in factories and other wartime roles did not come back to their attic bedrooms: the food may have been better in a country house but girls preferred the freedom of their new lives, without a housekeeper to poke into their rooms and stop them from seeing friends. Lutyens was somewhat above such considerations: he made few concessions to the new realities of domestic life. But they mattered to his potential clients, who were now being heavily taxed as the government struggled to pay for the war.

Amid all this, Lutyens's domestic life was falling apart. Relations with Emily had never been easy. Unresponsive to architecture, she was equally unresponsive to Ned as a husband, disliking his lovemaking so much that, once the five children had been born, she denied him her bed; and she had fallen hook, line and sinker for Theosophy, personified by the beautiful Krishnamurti. She travelled the world, preaching Labour politics and Indian Home Rule, in company with a ragged train of charlatans, paedophiles and defrocked priests. Lady Emily was not the only society figure to be intrigued by alternative religion: Pamela Tennant sought to contact the spirit world by table turning, prompting her sister-in-law

Margot Asquith to remark: 'I always knew the living talked rot, but it's nothing to the rot the dead talk.' After the First World War, bereft and desperate parents turned to spiritualism in the hope of contacting their dead sons. Even so, Emily's behaviour was extreme. 'She *is* a gloom,' wrote Harold Nicolson to his wife, Vita Sackville-West. After work Lutyens would play patience in an impenetrable silence which was barely broken at meals. Strangely, when apart from each other, they continued to write constantly, if not quite with the irrepressible fun of the old days; it was when they were under the same roof that words failed. That roof now belonged to a large house in Mansfield Street, Marylebone which Lutyens redecorated, putting new marble columns in the hall and painting the floor of the drawing room emerald green and the walls black. Despite the extravagance, he fretted about his profession going the same way as his father's. 'A woman may weep, a man bleeds,' he told Emily. Always anxious about money, he became more worried than ever.

Consolation came from Vita's lavishly spending mother Lady Sackville – MacSack. 'We seem to hit it off like he did with Miss Jekyll,' Sackville wrote in her diary. It was a perceptive observation: she had become another in the string of older women who helped his self-confidence and career. She was the antithesis of Emily: opulent, sophisticated, soft, rich, sexy, and married – for the time being – to a husband who let her do what she wanted. She told Lutyens to dress better, which he did, and stop punning so much, which he didn't. If sex ever reared its head, it did not do so for long. Architecture and decoration were the bond. While she was not quite so rich as Lutyens had thought, she was the ideal client, although he repaid her badly: his remodelling of three houses in Sussex Square, Brighton, to form a single dwelling stuffed with furniture from Knole was a rare failure: 'a bottomless pit absorbing at least £50,000 of MacSack's fortune,' as Jane Ridley puts it. But he needed the work. Eventually, when money ran short after her divorce and she became strange and paranoid, she obsessed about the expenses, accusing Lutyens of a host of wrongdoings, such as making off with her furniture. (Eventually she took Lutyens to court, but lost and had to pay him £150 for her 'malice'.) For now, she gave him a Rolls-Royce along with a chauffeur called James – to give him the satisfaction of being able to say, 'Home, James.'

A homage to the world that had vanished was made in the form of a dolls' house. The idea was born in 1920, when Queen Victoria's artistic granddaughter, Princess Marie Louise, former wife of the Kaiser's homosexual cousin Prince Aribert of Anhalt, agreed to ask Queen Mary if she would allow the making of one; it was to be given to the Queen – a lover of furniture, bibelots and intricate workmanship – when it was finished. When Lutyens got hold of the project, it grew and grew – in complexity if not in scale. It became not merely a dolls' house but an architectural model that minutely detailed the comfortable and civilised way of life that he and his clients had enjoyed before the First World War. This would be Lutyens's ideal house, a whimsy that – in the tradition of the follies in landscape parks – had a serious intent at its core. Lutyens found it completely engrossing; he guaranteed some of the cost of making it with his own money, which could have been ruinous for him. Here was a world made for children, designed by a man of child-like imagination, but which was far too precious for any real child to play with – a hymn of nostalgia for a golden era, made on a tiny scale to miraculous standards of craftsmanship; with, amongst the miniaturisation, numerous pieces of wit.

Three years after the completion of the Dolls' House, Le Corbusier would publish *Vers une architecture*, declaring that a house was a machine for living in. With limousines and motorcycles in the garage, a hydraulic lift, a motor mower for Gertrude Jekyll's garden and a tiny Bassett-Lowke model steam engine in the nursery, the Dolls' House perpetuates the Edwardian view that machines were essentially for playing with, and houses to be rich in craft. At Lutyens's grand new home at 13 Mansfield Street, Queen Mary – known in her family as May – would shyly ask for private time with it so she could be a girl again. The Dolls' House also inspired one of Lutyens's better jokes. When she asked why the pillowcases were embroidered with the initials MG and GM, he replied that one stood for 'May George?' and the other 'George May'.[9]

Had the Dolls' House been real, it might have met the fate of Devonshire House and other aristocratic town palaces in London, whose owners could not afford the taxation brought in to pay for the war: they were being demolished and replaced with offices or flats. It was an equally bleak era for the country house, although the catastrophe that spelt the doom of Park House at Mells was common to many country houses down the ages: on a blustery Somerset night, it caught fire. When summoned, the Frome Fire Brigade could not find horses, due to the number taken by the army, and the Radstock Fire Brigade's engine got stuck in mud. Meanwhile the wind whipped up the flames. Fortunately the contents were saved and moved to Mells Manor but the house itself was destroyed. Lutyens dreaded that the Horners would ask him to rebuild it, since, in the straitened conditions of the time, they might not have paid.

He need not have worried. Ideal clients would present themselves in 1923 – the McKennas. They took a twenty-five year lease on the ruin of Park House, Mells, in exchange for erecting a new dwelling. Before politics, McKenna had been a successful barrister but his income from the law could not have allowed him and Pamela to live high. This changed when he left the House of Commons; in 1919, he became Chairman of the Midland Bank, then the biggest bank in the world.

Sketches for Park House, Mells, rebuilt in 1922–3 by the Midland Bank chairman, Reginald McKenna, after a fire. Motors (bottom sketch) arrive at what used to be the back, so that visitors approach the house through a ruin garden formed out of Soane's old service yard.

There is a McKenna album in the Churchill Archives pasted with photographs of family and friends: Pamela and Barbara as girls in white dresses, with Gertrude Jekyll's painter friend, Hercules Brabazon Brabazon, at Munstead House; and Liberal luminaries who had been Reginald's parliamentary colleagues, such as Asquith and Churchill. Towards the back are Lutyens's first sketches for the reconstruction of Park House and photographs of work in progress. The latter show that nothing was kept of the main house beyond a single external wall. This gave Lutyens carte blanche to create a virtually new house, on the old foundations. Where the old house had two bays, Lutyens made the principal façade flat and threw a giant order of pilasters across it, after the manner of Lees Court in Kent (a house associated with Inigo Jones). Window shutters, of the kind he had used at Nashdom, add a French note. Far removed from the Surrey Style, shutters would become a signature of his late country houses, reappearing on Mothecombe, Middleton Park and Halnaker House; green was the colour often preferred, perhaps another memory of the Escorial. The stone blocks of the Gibbs surround of the door of Park House merge into the pilasters to either side, creating a Mannerist sense of ambiguity. Pure Lutyens – and so is the quirky brilliance of your arrival. Guests assume, as they bowl across the park, that the drive is heading straight for the door just described. Where would have been the romance in that? Instead, it bends sharply, taking a line to what had been the back of the house. You leave the car to follow a path that leads through a garden made out of the old dependencies. To either side are the arches of former cart sheds designed by Sir John Soane, forming a kind of cloister and framing Lutyens's grand doorway. Here is Ned playing the magician, for the effect is completely unexpected: a tour de force of the aesthetic movement known as the Picturesque, which saw beauty in ruins and valued them for the associations they evoked. The arrangement was also practical because the McKennas' car stopped next to the garage; in the age of the horse, stables had been kept at arm's length because of the smell. Lutyens sent McKenna a parcel of Indian woods, presumably for the interior: a reflection of his knowledge of the subcontinent and half a world away from the ubiquitous oak of Munstead Wood. The drawing room contained two pianos for Pamela and her musical friends. Having been presented with silver trowels for assistance rendered to the workmen building Park House, the McKenna boys, Michael and David, who were at Eton, spent their summers on long expeditions, bathing, sailing with their father, or riding out to the 'steep green terraces and scented elder groves' of Cadbury Castle (taken to be Camelot) or Glastonbury Tor.[10]

McKenna did not stand in the 1918 general election; instead he surprised his political friends by succeeding Sir Edward Holden, who died in 1919, as Chairman of the Midland Bank. This was a piece of luck for Lutyens, busy with war memorials and cemeteries and still finishing New Delhi, but whose practice had yet to find a new direction in the changed circumstances of the peace. He would receive four commissions from the Midland in the 1920 and 1930s, beginning with 196a Piccadilly – the jewel of a building described in chapter 6 – in 1922 and reaching a triumphant climax in the titanic palace of commerce that was the Midland's headquarters building in Poultry, in the City of London, not absolutely complete (following an extension) until the fateful year of 1939.

196a Piccadilly was a branch building – an important one, from its position in the West End, as a result of which the Midland hoped that foreign visitors to the 'hotel, theatre and shopping district' would give it their business: upstairs there was an oak-panelled Visitors' Room where customers could transact business, write letters or 'pass a quiet hour in reading'.[11] To C. Lewis Hind, writing his 'Life and I' column in the *Daily Chronicle*, 'this delightful, red brick and white stone garlanded building' was an advertisement in architecture, saying to wayfarers: 'Here is a great corporation willing to forgo the rents from sky-scraping offices, eager to place on a valuable site a small building, sufficient to their needs, content in the knowledge that they are preserving the beauty of London.'[12] The premises had been designed, inside and out, by the bank's usual architects, Whinney, Son and Austen Hall, but when board approval was sought, the chairman declared that the Midland could do better. Lutyens redesigned the exterior and supplied the early Georgian ceiling, while the more bankerly aspects were left to Whinney, Son and Austen Hall. Lutyens's other Midland commissions were also collaborations, either with them or with Gotch and Saunders of Kettering, founded by John Alfred Gotch, author of *Early Renaissance Architecture in England* as well as books on Northamptonshire houses and Inigo Jones, who served as President of the Royal Institute of British Architects in 1923–5.

Midland Bank, Poultry. 1920s London needed far bigger buildings than those of the Victorian period. Lutyens's Elemental Classicism eschews ornament in favour of geometry, with a fractional reduction in the height of the rustication bands as they rise up the building.

This Midland Bank branch in Piccadilly was designed to attract visitors to London. Next to the church of St James's, Piccadilly, it gave Lutyens the opportunity to challenge Wren. His design is inspired by Sanmicheli.

When McKenna became chairman, the bank had over four-teen hundred branches. Most had been acquired as part of the consolidation of numerous small local banks of the Victorian era: already the market was dominated by five large banks led by the Midland. But five hundred and twenty of those Midland branches were entirely new. The premises built for them had to look solid, solvent and rooted: Georgian was the preferred style. Holden had no doubt that architecture was a worthwhile invest-ment. 'In modern days', he told a shareholders' meeting in 1919, 'it is absolutely necessary to have good bank premises, because a good bank with poor premises does not attract deposits in the same way as a bank with good premises.'[13] At one point, the Midland asked Lutyens to design a template for branch-building, although it was never introduced due to the differing circumstances of each site and branch. The variety can be seen from Lutyens's own commissions. While 196a Piccadilly is domestic in scale, his branches in Leadenhall Street and Manchester were large and stone-faced, and his mighty Midland headquarters in Poultry was a commercial leviathan.

Lutyens had already turned his mind to the challenge of tall, monumental buildings for big corporations. In 1920 he was com-missioned to build a headquarters for the Anglo-Persian Oil Company (later BP) on Finsbury Circus, in the City of London. Like the two petrol pumps in the Dolls' House – one for Shell and another for Pratts, which became Esso – it was evidence that the new age would run on petrol rather than hay.

Finsbury Circus had been laid out as an elliptical park in 1810. The curve may have turned Lutyens's thoughts to the Italian Baroque, and from that to the Mannerism of the six-teenth century, specifically Palladio's most Mannerist building, the Loggia del Capitaniato in Vicenza, and Michelangelo's Laurentian Library. Britannic House shows that the wheels of the world were turning again. They were powered not only by petrol but by finance.

Postwar reconstruction was good for banks. The banks in turn required buildings. Baker got the job of enlarging the Bank of England in 1921. Most of the Big Five clearing banks commissioned new head offices nearby. For the Midland head office, around the corner from the Bank of England, within a stone's throw of the Mansion House and convenient for livery halls and other City institutions, Lutyens produced a palace of finance comparable (as A.S.G. Butler wrote in the *Memorial Volumes*) to the palace he designed for the Viceroy in New Delhi. It stood on a complex site that ran between Prince's Street and Poultry, partly inherited from the London Joint Stock Bank with which the Midland amalgamated in 1918; a heritage row erupted after the bank acquired the graveyard of a vanished chapel to extend the Poultry frontage, and construction was interrupted when it was found that the subterranean River Walbrook ran underneath the new edifice. The building itself gives no hint of these difficulties. In 1924, work began on a composition of astonishing breadth and assurance. While the Viceroy's House created a new kind of Classicism, fusing the Western tradition with ideas from the East, the Midland Bank head office goes further – almost beyond the conventional Classical repertoire altogether. The enormous volume is controlled not by columns but simple arches arranged in bands. The lower two bands form a base, above which rises a smaller façade with the corners cut off. Across the whole front of Portland stone run channels of rustication; the onlooker may not realise it, but the rustication has been the subject of minute calculations so that each block is slightly smaller than the one below it. This creates a barely perceptible batter, so that the great mass of masonry not only seems even bigger than it really is, due to the false perspective, but comes alive. Although the diminution was minuscule – .273 recurring of an inch – Lutyens's assistants had to draw it precisely. As one of them recalled, Lutyens

> would admit of no approximation in the drawings, on the plea that plenty of inaccuracies would creep in without beginning in the office. 'About! I don't know what you mean by "about",' he would say. At any time he was prepared to alter his fundamental unit if he saw a better, thereby jettisoning all drawings to date and thereby causing all-night last-minute 'panics' in the office.[14]

The windows also diminish slightly in size the higher up they are. When McKenna observed that the keystones to the fourth floor windows, which were individually carved, could not be distinguished at street level, Lutyens replied: 'Reggie, if you stood at a fourth floor window with some of your clerks, do you think I would not recognise your face?' He won his point.[15]

The head office is not entirely without ornament: there are columns in antis to mark the entrance on Poultry; statues of boys with geese – a reference to Poultry, or possibly the geese that lay the golden eggs – at the cut-off corners; aedicules; obelisks; and over the whole, for those who can see it, is a dome, like a smaller version of that on the Viceroy's House. 'The effect of this virtuosity', wrote Christopher Hussey, 'is that the whole elevation is vibrant with life … We can see in it, besides, Lutyens's transition from Classical to Elemental architecture taking place.'[16] Walls seem to dissolve and reconstitute themselves, making this the most thrilling of all rusticated façades in the world, beating even those of the Pitti Palace in Florence.

Inside the building, customers were treated to a large and luxurious banking hall decorated with green verdite columns and pilasters and lit by a central overhead lantern, the black and white patterned floor echoing those of Lutyens's country houses in the 1920s.

A ceiling from Devonshire House, then being demolished, was removed and stored in the Old Kent Road, presumably intended for use in the boardroom although not installed. The Midland followed the Poultry head office by commissioning new branches by Lutyens for Leadenhall Street – a narrow site – and King Street, Manchester, where the island site enabled him to create a building with three nearly identical façades, in the elemental style of Poultry. As the staff magazine put it,

> The design of the exterior ... has been developed in an interesting manner with a series of steppings and set backs, so that in spite of its massive size and height the building never appears

The enormous banking hall of the Midland Bank, Poultry, created for an age in which all banking transactions were paper-based. It has adapted surprisingly well to its new use as a dining space for the many restaurants of The Ned hotel.

out of scale or heavy, while the simple treatment of the main wall surfaces affords that pleasing modern effect so desirable in an up-to-date office building.[17]

Both Leadenhall Street and King Street, Manchester, are faced in Portland stone.

The Leadenhall Street branch was not commissioned until 1929, the year of the Wall Street Crash. This was late. To quote the hundred-and-fifty-year history of the Midland Bank published in 1986, 'Most of the City's splendid banking halls had been planned early in the 1920s, when hopes for the future of the domestic economy were still running high.' By the time they were ready for occupation, Britain was in the grip of a depression, forcing a financial crisis that only ended with the abandonment of the gold standard.

> The new headquarters of the banks, instead of serving as tranquil surroundings for hospitality for customers and international bankers, were the scene of emergency meetings, attempts to rescue major customers, and fierce arguments over reconstruction agreements.[18]

The Midland's palace of finance may have seemed no more appropriate for its time than a Viceroy's Palace completed when India was on the verge of Independence. It is notable, however, that both are superbly maintained, the Midland in its new incarnation as The Ned, named after Lutyens.

TWELVE

THE BIGGEST DOME IN CHRISTENDOM

Metropolitan Cathedral, Liverpool 1929–41

Design of the mighty stone pulpit of the Roman Catholic Metropolitan Cathedral of Christ the King. The drawing is enlivened by the figure of a cardinal preaching a fiery sermon.

'THE RECEIPT OF YOUR KIND LETTER GAVE ME THE moment of my life.' Lutyens wrote these words on July 9, 1929 to Archbishop Richard Downey who had just asked him to design Liverpool Metropolitan Cathedral. The commission had an extraordinary effect on him. While neither he nor Emily was conventionally religious, and certainly not Catholic, he was conscious of getting old. The world of his clients had lost its buoyancy. His concentration on things of the soul – however much he rejected the teachings of the church – seems to have fed the mystic side of his being. This man who was always anxious about money charged no fee for his work (perhaps believing he would never get paid). Here was a sacrifice at the altar of one obvious god: Architecture. Perhaps other less obvious subjects of belief were involved: Lutyens's inner workings are not easy to read. It only truly revealed itself through his designs.

Christopher Hussey was in no doubt about the importance of the commission. Describing the drawings exhibited at the Royal Academy in 1932 he wrote: 'it is not exaggeration to say [that it] surpasses in grandeur any project exhibited by the Academy since its foundation, or, indeed, any Christian church designed by a single architect'. Like the Viceroy's House, conceived when the Imperial sun was still high in the sky but not finished until it was disappearing below the horizon, the cathedral seems out of its time – Baroque oratorio in an age that was moving increasingly towards twelve-tone serialism. Liverpool, as the great town planner and head of Architecture at Liverpool University, Professor Charles Reilly wrote in *Country Life*, was 'certainly not at the most flourishing epoch of her career'. Her heyday as the port that linked Great Britain and the United States, first for merchant ships, including those that carried slaves on one leg of the triangular trade, and more recently the glamorous ocean liners that financed the construction of the Cunard Building – one of the Three Graces on the Pier Head – and the Adelphi Hotel was over. In 1907 the White Star Line's express ships were transferred to Southampton which was closer to London and could take larger vessels: it was from there that the Titanic sailed for America in 1912. Decline was followed by slump, with a worldwide recession. Lutyens felt it too. Work had dried up, old clients like Herbert Johnson were telling the footman to lay the table in the dark to save electricity (he sold Marsh Court at

In Lutyens's characteristic worm's-eye view sketch, the great triumphal arch that he conceived as the narthex to his cathedral in Liverpool rears up dramatically. Heated and with lavatories concealed in the piers, it was to have provided night shelter for the homeless.

a loss); MacSack had lost her fortune and become fixated on the amount of money she (wrongly) thought Lutyens owed her. But recessions pass. This building would take decades to build and would stand for hundreds of years. Strangely, press criticism of the design was muted.

It was as though even potential doomsters were cowed by the scale of the ambition. Provision was made for a congregation of 10,000 souls. 'Sir Edwin's cathedral really is Brobdingnagian,' wrote the author of an *Observer* interview with Lutyens in 1933. Just as the Viceroy's House had outdone Versailles, so, according to the *Observer*, presumably on information obtained from the architect, the footprint of Liverpool would have exceeded that of St Peter's in Rome – 233,000 square feet as opposed to 227,000. Perhaps for reasons of tact, this was reduced to the 216,500 square feet cited by Jane Ridley. Still, the dome was to have been bigger than that of St Peter's, and St Paul's in London would have been dwarfed. It was to have risen over a city already rich in Classical architecture and to have been visible for miles. How many miles exactly, did the architect suppose? 'From America, I should think,' replied Sir Edwin to the *Observer* journalist. [1]

It occupied a triumphant position on Brownlow Hill, beetling over the surrounding terraces. There was an unspoken rivalry with the enormous Anglican cathedral at the other end of Liverpool's Hope Street, then being raised to the design of Sir Giles Gilbert Scott. Lutyens was pleased to discover that his site was thirty feet higher than that of Scott's cathedral. While Scott's Gothic design had a relatively simple silhouette which would read well from the sea – a cross with a rectangular tower at the centre – Lutyens's was to be rich and complex, ballooning in a glorious display of Classical richness to a dizzying height. Even to dream of a building of this scale is an extraordinary act of imagination. But perhaps not so strange to the early twentieth century as it might seem today.

Cathedrals had been built in the recent past – notably Westminster Cathedral, the external shell of which was raised quickly although the decoration of the internal domes remains unfinished to this day. Guildford Cathedral would not be begun until 1936; it was opened in 1965. Traditionally cathedrals have rarely been finished in the lifetime of the people who began them. Lutyens predicted that his might take centuries.

Great architecture, Lutyens had written, demanded great patrons. At Liverpool Lutyens found one in Archbishop Downey. In outward appearance – particularly until a crash diet caused this person of 5ft 4ins and strong will to lose half his body weight of 18 stone in a year – he could have come from the court of the Medici or Henry VIII. Born in Kilkenny, he was a cosmopolitan prelate, persuasive, proselytising and adored by his flock in Liverpool. Attempts had been made to build a Catholic cathedral in recognition of the half a million Irish people who had come to Liverpool after the Famine of 1849: restrictions on worship had been removed by the Catholic Emancipation Act of 1829, so a site was identified in Everton and the Roman Catholic architect E.W. Pugin, son of the leading propagandist for the Gothic Revival A.W.N. Pugin, was approached to design it, but funds were diverted and only the Lady Chapel was ever built. The absence of a cathedral in Liverpool became all the more keenly felt after it was declared the centre of an archdiocese in 1911. Downey's predecessor, Archbishop Keating, could do no more than identify a site, in the nine acres that were covered by a redundant warehouse, on a high point overlooking the city. The Orange Order bitterly opposed this being bought for a Catholic place of worship – and the cost was an obstacle too. At least the Slump made the land easier to acquire.

From the chaos of poverty and sickness, rises the shrine of Christ the King. From the carcass of misery and despondency come forth love and mercy. This is your Cathedral Church upon a workhouse site.

So wrote Lutyens to Downey, playing him with customary skill. But here was a client only too eager to build, with a salesmanship equal to Lutyens's own. He campaigned for funds under the slogan: 'A cathedral in our time'.

As Lutyens's son Robert wrote when the plans were being reconsidered after Lutyens's death, 'it was always Archbishop Downey's conviction that a church is a place with which, and not only in which, to worship God.'[2] In this the great cathedral would have been like the temples of Ancient Greece, which were not only places where offering to the gods could take place but were themselves an offering, built to be as permanent and beautiful as possible. This had also been the mindset of the Middle Ages when cathedrals and churches were far more richly decorated than private houses.

Faith, architecture and Downey's charisma came together in the stone-laying ceremony on Whit Monday, June 5, 1933. Lutyens erected a temporary high altar, with a baldacchino hung with stylised drapery made of wood. Statues of saints stood at the angles as they would on the cathedral, while above them, in the blazing sky, towered a figure of Christ the King. The ceremony was attended by two cardinals, forty bishops and a crowd of twenty-five thousand in the enclosure itself and more thousands outside. The little streets at the bottom of Brownlow Hill had been transformed by their inhabitants, who had hung them with white and gold paper, 'so that from a short distance the street seemed to be roofed in bands of ordered flowers, which threw grateful shadows upon the swept roadways'.[3] It was so hot that the road surface melted and, on Brownlow Hill, had to be sprayed with water to keep it hard enough to use. It must have reminded Lutyens of New Delhi. When the stone – a large block of granite – was winched into position, the entire congregation rose and 'cheered again and again, and clapped and waved flags and favours in the air'.

Whereas the Anglican cathedral is built of local sandstone, which Lutyens admitted to have 'a most beautiful colour', the Metropolitan Cathedral would be constructed from brick, largely hand-made and dressed with the most enduring of building stones, granite. This dictated the form. Like the Thiepval Arch, it was to be massively rectangular, a composition of blocks and voids that played symphonic variations on the triumphal arch. The walls would have been battered and cliff-like, with few windows. They rose, by a thrilling geometrical progression, to the immense dome, which was to have been of an elemental character – a hemisphere rising from a plain drum. This would have been unlike any dome previously built, in that there was no ring of columns or entablature beneath it; the only comparison is with the supercolossal sphere that the French Revolutionary architect Boullée designed as an imaginary cenotaph for Newton. Four Y-shaped projections from the storey below the dome would have formed the transition between the circle of the dome and the rectangular plan of the cathedral. The skyline would have been enlivened with pavilion-like structures conceived in the language of Lutyens's war memorials. They would have been joined by columns bearing statues of saints – of the kind seen in Italy, where the Church reused columns carved by the Romans. The complexity of silhouette is reminiscent of Hagia Sophia in Istanbul.

The term narthex usually means a vestibule or porch. At Liverpool, the narthex became a major structure in its own right, a huge space that, with superb symbolism, was big enough to shelter the homeless poor. The floor was to have been heated and lavatories included within the piers. The east end of the cathedral was to have consisted of a huge plain wall, hung with escutcheons in the manner of a palazzo. Above it were two domes with spires derived from Wren's design for Old St Paul's.

Alas, Lutyens's Liverpool cathedral did not rise above the crypt but this model was made in 1929 to raise funds. Following the Thiepval Arch and inspired by the ruins of Ancient Rome, the cathedral's principal material would have been brick.

There was to have been no iron in the building, only a girdle of stainless steel around the drum of the dome. Iron would have eventually perished. This was to have been a building to have lasted through the millennia, leaving, at the end perhaps, a spectacular ruin, somewhat like the Baths of Caracalla whose plan it resembles – or more optimistically, continuing to amaze visitors as one of the Wonders of the World, like Hagia Sophia. It was not to be: the project changed after the Second World War, before morphing into something that was the antithesis of Lutyens's design – not a reaffirmation of eternal truths in a new guise so much as a popular icon to appeal to the 1960s. But the model of the cathedral that was made to raise funds can be seen in the Museum of Liverpool on the Pier Head, in sparkling condition after thirteen years of restoration. Although exhibited in Dublin, the model was not of great use in raising money because it was too big to transport, but it remains a mighty if somewhat poignant object. Weighing twenty tons, it took twelve craftsmen two years to bring to its present state of completion – although still far short of what Lutyens envisaged. After £5,000 had been spent, the diocese refused to commit the further £6,500 that Lutyens estimated was needed to finish it.

Inside the cathedral, Lutyens allowed little for decoration beyond that provided by the structure. Perhaps his fingers had been burnt by St Jude's, Hampstead Garden Suburb, where the programme of painted scenes with which Walter Starmer covered the domes, vaults, apse and Lady Chapel in the 1920s could be regarded as a distraction. All, at Liverpool, would lie in the volumes and vistas – made the more dramatic by the need to pierce the giant piers supporting the dome in two directions so that (as required from the beginning) the whole congregation could see the high altar. There were dramatic effects of hidden lighting. The structure supporting the dome had been better conceived than that of St Paul's, where Wren resorted to arches of different widths. An innovation was to have been an organ set below ground so that its sound mingled harmoniously with that of the choir – an idea already tried on a smaller scale in the Temple of Music at Tyringham. The walls would have been lined with travertine, the nave floor made from dark silver-coloured cast iron, the raised portions of the floor laid with marble. Beyond this restrained palette there would have been no other colour except for that provided by the altar cloths and priests' vestments, which Lutyens designed himself.

Speaking to the *Observer*, Lutyens would not commit himself to a timetable for constructing the cathedral. 'It will depend on how fast the money comes in and, again, on how building costs move in the future. This will decide whether we shall be fifty years or 250 years.' It might have been finished in twenty years if a benefactor had produced three million pounds. No such fairy godmother was forthcoming, however. Only the crypt was constructed – although that is enough to provide a glimpse of the wonders of which the world was deprived when building stopped after the Second World War. It is big enough to contain several churches. Dark charcoal brick and bands of stone are the only materials of the walling. The effect is sombre but mesmerising, and the quality of the bricklaying as good as that of Lutyens's Surrey period. Off the great vaulted space of the Pontifical Hall, used for services while the cathedral was being built but ultimately intended for use by priests as they robed, are two chapels made from travertine, entered by doorcases of abstract and ambiguous form, more a geometrical puzzle than a conventional composition with columns. There are sarcophagi over the doorcases, and a hint of Giulio Romano's Palazzo del Te in Mantua in the way that the keystones over the doors slip downwards. While Castle Drogo has a working portcullis, the Chapel of Relics was given a gate in the form of a six-ton disc of stone. This is rolled into position to protect the relics but, since it is made to an openwork pattern of different symbols, allows visitors to peer in. The rolling stone evokes the stone that sealed Christ's tomb until rolled away by angels at the Resurrection.

Either the cathedral changed Lutyens or it brought to the surface a spirituality that he had long concealed beneath his jokes. One night he walked back to Mansfield Street with his former pupil Andy Butler – the A.S.G. Butler who would analyse his designs in the *Memorial Volumes* published after Lutyens's death – to see the model, which filled the drawing room. Butler found it 'an extraordinarily moving experience, because for once at least he was deadly serious, and kept asking me whether I liked this and that, with an enchanting humility'.[4]

The Liverpool Metropolitan Cathedral would have been a great work of twentieth-century Classicism, in a language that was

The Chapel of Relics in the crypt of the cathedral shows the elements of Classicism being reduced to their barest essentials in Lutyens's last years. A three-ton door made from stone quarried on site can be rolled out, recalling the stone that sealed Christ's tomb.

entirely of the age: austere and invented by Lutyens, and yet related to the glories of the Ancient past, whose vocabulary it uses. It would have been a magnificent contribution to a city that already possessed many great works of Classicism, from St George's Hall by C.R. Cockerell to Mewes and Davis's Cunard Building on the Pier Head. Against that, the effort to build it is not remembered with universal affection. Lutyens might be criticised for luring rich clients to spend more than they intended – but each month the Diocese of Liverpool's wheedling priests extracted a thousand pounds from parishioners who sometimes struggled to feed their families. And just as the Viceroy's House was built for an empire going into eclipse, so the cathedral was imagined for a city whose fortunes were already waning. The Mersey Tunnel was opened in 1934 so that the people of Birkenhead could work in Liverpool but would soon be facilitating a reverse flow, as anyone with money escaped an increasingly moribund city. The efforts of the Luftwaffe during the Second World War were compounded by labour unrest, reducing Liverpool to a state of civic implosion from which not even Beatlemania could rescue it. Then the Roman Catholic Church itself shed its old skin following the Second Vatican Council of the early 1960s. The liturgy and splendour beloved of Archbishop Downey were replaced by *versus populum* – masses said facing the congregation. Lutyens's design was revised by Adrian Scott, then abandoned completely in favour of a competition. This was won by Sir Frederick Gibberd and a centrally planned church surmounted by a crown – Paddy's Wigwam, in popular parlance – was the result. It would be easy to sneer. Gibberd's cathedral is popular with those who use it. Writing of the model in *Country Life*, Christopher Hussey called Lutyens's cathedral 'one of the most Romantic buildings ever conceived'. Alas, Romance was dead.[5]

THIRTEEN

WHY NOT
ASK ME?

Campion Hall, Oxford 1935–7

Lutyens converted a blot on a letter he was writing to Father D'Arcy into the figure of a saint, with halo and cross. 'I apologise for the Blot. I *have* blessed it!' he wrote.

T OWARDS THE END OF HIS LIFE, LUTYENS RECEIVED his last major commission: Campion Hall in Oxford. Whether by luck or intention, it gave him the opportunity to reprise several of the important themes of his career, being a blend of the Surrey Arts and Crafts of his early period – a trifle more Spartan, perhaps, but then he had never been much of a one for comfort – and the geometrical language that he had developed for the war memorials and Liverpool Cathedral. He even inserted the Delhi Order, part of a riff on bells which had a specific reference to those using the building. It was the centre of the Jesuits in Oxford.

Before 1871 Oxford had been a Protestant university but its doors had been opened by the University Tests Act. Even so, it was only at the end of the century that the English hierarchy of the Roman Catholic Church thought it safe for Roman Catholics to attend. First on the scene had been the Jesuits, who opened Pope's Hall – named after its master Thomas Pope, SJ – in 1896. It was a small establishment, next to the Lamb and Flag public house, which, by the 1930s, seemed inadequate both to the numbers of Catholics at the University and the image that the Masters of Campion Hall – as Pope's Hall had become – wanted to project. The master from 1933 was the charismatic Father Martin D'Arcy. D'Arcy, who had been teaching at Oxford since 1927, was England's leading apologist for Roman Catholicism, concentrating his efforts at conversion on an intellectual and social elite: successes included Evelyn Waugh and Graham Greene. The artist Stanley Parker described his etiolated features as appearing 'wasted to the bone by the rarest and most exquisite emotions, seared with the imprint of the deepest thought, consumed, almost, by the inner fire which blazed and smouldered in his eyes'. Alas, Parker was not up to capturing these qualities in his paint, but Augustus John provides a memorable if not wholly lifelike portrait: penetrating dark eyes beneath a triangular frizz of hair appear disconcertingly in a face as thin as a knife-blade. As Master, D'Arcy inherited the intention to build a new hall from his predecessor, as well as an architect in the shape of E. Bower Norris. Norris had not impressed the Jesuit fathers, and D'Arcy added to the ignominy in which he was held by asking the manager of Claridge's to opine on the lavatories; as he had suspected, they were inadequate.

It was Frances Horner from Mells who advised him to take an opinion from Lutyens. Then in his mid sixties, Ned was recognised to be, in the words of the beadle or head of the junior common room, 'the greatest architect of the British Empire'. On reviewing Norris's plans, Lutyens found them wanting, but Norris refused to meet him to talk through the objections, stung, perhaps, by criticism of a design that leant heavily on the precedent of the Hall in Bradford-on-Avon, the very building that Lutyens himself had reprised for his pavilion at the Paris Exposition Universelle of 1900. This left D'Arcy without an architect and he sought help from Lutyens, who said: 'Why not ask me?' The reply was to the point. 'But Ned, you have the reputation of being most appallingly expensive.'[1] Lutyens assured him that his fees would be minimal and that he would keep an eye on the cost. This was not a client he would take to the cleaners. And so Ned entered the esoteric, socially glamorous world of Jesuit Oxford, where architectural austerity would be combined with high art to form a haunt for, among others, Evelyn Waugh.

As D'Arcy later wrote, not only had Lutyens been appointed to design Liverpool's Metropolitan Cathedral, which would have rivalled St Peter's in Rome if it had risen above crypt level, but he 'regarded as the greatest architect of the British Empire'.[2]

In all his long career, Lutyens had only built once in the ancient universities – a single range of what had started as a three-sided scheme at Magdalene College, Cambridge, overlooking the River Cam. Campion Hall, although technically a permanent private hall, was tantamount to being a college. This must have been an attraction, even if the long, narrow site on Brewer Street – the best of the three under consideration – was restricted: no grand entrance

Brewer Street is too narrow to allow more than a series of recessed arches to enhance the entrance. Restraint is the key to Lutyens's work throughout Campion Hall.

would be possible since it could only be seen at an angle. In addition to which, Christ Church, which owned the land, and the Oxford Preservation Trust were both anxious that Micklem Hall, an old building on Brewer Street which formed part of the Campion Hall site, should not be demolished; incorporating it into the façade added another picturesque note. But the architect of the Viceroy's House in New Delhi and Liverpool Cathedral could dispense with grandeur. He made a virtue of restraint, in a building that combines the Arts and Crafts simplicity of his early country houses with the geometry that he regarded as eternal and close to divine.

In June 1934, Father Leslie Walker, who was tasked with supervising the project, could write: 'Your plans have not only been approved by Rome, but have been described as "excellent".' Among the various suggestions made for improvement only one was deemed essential: the inclusion of a central staircase, which the fathers were also unanimous in wanting.

In plan Campion Hall is an L, the two wings of which enclose a garden; Lutyens had intended that another L would be added to create a quad but this never happened. For the elevations, he rose above the bad blood that had existed between him and Sir Herbert Baker over New Delhi and borrowed his palette of materials from Rhodes House, which Baker had completed six years before. These were Bladon rubble stone and Clipsham ashlar, the latter being more resistant to weathering than the traditional ashlar from Headington. The style is loosely Tudor. Standing on narrow Brewer Street, the entrance takes the form of a recessed arch with archivolts, reminiscent of the garden front at Deanery Garden: a preparation for the domestic tone of the interior. There is only a row of small windows on the ground floor and a row of tripartite chapel windows to the second floor to relieve the otherwise blank wall of masonry, giving something of the character of a Florentine palazzo. The northeast corner, next to Christ Church Cathedral School, is more volumetric:

the apse of the chapel rises above another blank wall with a loggia on the ground floor. But this elides with a block of domestic character with gables and mullion windows. To the other side of this block is the garden front, occupying the long stroke of the L. Here the windows create a syncopated rhythm, those on the top and bottom storeys being roughly (and not always) aligned, while the ones on the middle floor are centred on the intervening spaces.

The theme of the interior is white walls and wood: oak for the floors, teak for the staircases. The staircases have a massive character. In the entrance hall, the main stair – Lutyens's response to the request from Rome – rises on broad treads with turned balusters to the side. The south stair has no balusters, only panelled

Originally designed to be part of a quadrangle, the open garden comes as quite a surprise after the narrow street beyond. One side is occupied by the old Micklem Hall, which Lutyens was asked to retain as part of his design. The doorcase uses the order he invented for New Delhi.

sides, economical but dramatic. The stylised bells that decorate the newel posts of the main stair make reference to the bells that rang throughout the day, calling the Order to prayer. This also excused Lutyens's use of the Delhi Order to the doorcase on the garden front: stone bells hang from the corners.

One of the two big rooms on the garden front is the library. Bookstacks rise to the ceiling, to create bays with desks. Several librarians had advised that shelves should be no longer than three feet to avoid sagging. There would be blocks, painted black with numbers in white: 'I should like to have them painted by a body who can do beautiful lettering,' wrote Lutyens, alarmed that Walker thought the painting could have been done by the fathers. Originally, some of Lutyens's spider-back chairs were drawn up to the desks but the design probably proved too fragile for college use and at some point they were replaced. The upper shelves of the bookcases are reached by ingenious library steps – a work of geometry in themselves.

Next to the library is the refectory or dining hall: plain, as befits a religious order, though beautiful in its simplicity. Mullion windows overlook the garden, opposite is a fireplace in a bolection surround – the austerity is relieved only by a plaster rose in the centre of the ceiling, because the fathers dined *sub rosa* (in secrecy). Not even the Jesuits could repress Lutyens's love of jokes. To either side of the entrance door are stands with pigeonholes for the fathers' napkins.

Given the discipline of the Order, the luxuries of the table, when allowed, were recorded by successive beadles in Beadle's Books: the boxes in which they are kept still smell of tobacco. The opening of the Hall on June 26, 1936 was accompanied by a tea served on a table that ran the length of the garden front, as well as small tables in the library: 'strawberries numerous & excellent'. The guests, who included the Duke of Alba and Berwick, Lutyens,

Waugh, Frances Horner, some heads of colleges, Catholic aristoc-racy and the rector of the Catholic school, Stonyhurst, 'formed a most brilliant company'. Hilary Term 1937 opened with 'Glass of port at dinner. Cig after dinner'. On January 18, D'Arcy 'lectured in the new Hall in the lecture-room for the first time to-day', to 90 people. Two days later the beadle listed some of the works of art that had been given to the Hall, to which could be added 'the great beauty and efficiency of the new Hall, which is due to the initiative of the Master in securing Sir Edwin Lutyens, the greatest architect in England, as architect'. After dinner, guests who repaired to the senior common room, formed from an early Georgian panelled room in Micklem Hall, were in for a surprise: Lutyens had done the walls in black lacquer, while the ceiling was green. Black is a clerical colour but it also provided an appropriately dark background, evocative of the ambience of a northern recusant manor house, for the hanging of pictures of Stuart monarchs and pretenders. This striking scheme has since been painted out in favour of more conventional colours.

Evelyn Waugh celebrated the Hospitality of Campion Hall in a manuscript reminiscence kept in the Hall's archive:

> We came from all quarters as guests of the house; fellows and undergraduates, gowned, from the neighbouring colleges, ref-ugees from foreign tyranny, editors of Catholic papers from London, under-Secretaries of State visiting the Chatham or the Canning, the President of the Royal Academy, the Spanish Ambassador, and men marked by no notoriety but distinguished by the high privilege of the Master's friendship. You never knew whom you would meet at Campion Hall but one thing was certain, that for a single evening at any rate they would all fit harmoniously into the social structure which the Master, without apparent effort, ingeniously contrived.

While today the Hall may feel pleasantly and appropriately severe, that is not the impact it had on Waugh in the 1930s. Accommodation across Oxford was Spartan. So Waugh felt

> it was remarkable that the only religious house in the university should appear less monastic than the secular colleges … the carpeted entrance-hall, the broad staircase, the profusion of ornate furniture, the bed-rooms with their tasteful choice of bed-side books, the prodigality and accessibility of hot-water, all had the air of a private house rather than of a college; they charmed visitors from the grimmer cloisters of the Continent and sometimes rather disconcerted the many newcomers for whom Campion Hall provided the first acquaintance with conventual life.

Once the Hall had been completed, D'Arcy began on what he called his Treasure Hunt. Due to (relative) poverty, Prince Rupert of Bavaria, the last heir apparent to the Bavarian throne, was selling the travelling altar that had belonged to Mary, Queen of Scots. He bought it, probably at a good price. It would be the first of many works of art and pieces of historical interest that would adorn the building. D'Arcy's budget may have been modest but his charm and powers of persuasion went far. There would be early Renaissance chasubles bought from an Italian refugee, chalices secured with the help of an Armenian Jew, gorgeous cloth of gold robes from China decorated with dragons and birds – which a nun seamstress easily transformed into a chasuble by slitting the armpits and adding 'a small gold cross at the back'. A Franco-Burgundian chasuble, which experts judged to be one of the finest vestments of the Middle Ages to have come onto the market, was bought at auction after the Second World War: the lots had been so badly displayed that few dealers had noticed it – except for one who said he would not bid against D'Arcy. Similarly, Sir Kenneth Clark, as he then was, wrote to say that he had hoped to buy a Crucifixion, drawn by Michelangelo and painted by his assistant Venusti; he stopped bidding as soon as he saw D'Arcy's hand go up: a religious house was 'the most appropriate place for such a beautiful painting'.

One spectacular work was contributed, indirectly, by Lutyens. Before boarding a liner at Southampton to go to New York, D'Arcy had lunch with his architect, and as they waited for the food to arrive, the latter pulled out a photograph of a seventeenth-century Spanish carving. The owner had wondered if it would be suitable for Lutyens's Liverpool Cathedral, the crypt of which was then being built. D'Arcy immediately recognised it as depicting St Ignatius, almost lifesize, with (on their knees) his followers, and snaffled it for Campion Hall. Opposite the foot of the main staircase, it became one of the most prominent of the Hall's many treasures. Fitted into the wall of the staircase is a plaque of St Martin in modern military dress from the studio of Eric Gill. The features of the beggar to whom he gives the cloak are supposedly those of D'Arcy.

As the focus of life at Campion Hall, the chapel became a work of art in itself. Lutyens had created, on the first floor, a spatially simple space, Romanesque in character: a single cell covered by a barrel vault. Restraint added to the beauty. A central aisle paved in black and white (slate and Portland stone) leads to the altar, whose baldacchino is a smaller relative of the one Lutyens designed for the Catholic Cathedral in Liverpool. Reaching nearly to the top of the vault, itself 27ft high, it is powerful but not overwhelming. Here the Delhi order, which features on the doorcase to Campion Hall's garden front, reappears. Another reminiscence of the Viceroy's House comes in the form of the light fittings: discs of pale blue glass suspended from cords but with the added detail of a tassel, making them into cardinal's hats. (Since Jesuits cannot become cardinals, they are hung so high as to be out of reach.) Joke or not, the delicacy of the fittings adds charm to the otherwise plain interior. There is only one colour accent, apart from the recent introduction of a painting of the risen Christ and Mary Magdalene behind the altar: the wave-like beam at the end of oak pews was painted in what Arthur Oswald, describing Campion Hall in *Country Life* on June 27, 1936, called sealing-wax red. Lutyens said it should be like his blood but it was a witticism too far: he wrote to apologise the next day. In the panelling to the side are set Frank Brangwyn's lithographs of the Stations of the Cross, printed onto thin sheets of wood and originally made for Arras Cathedral; they were presented by the artist.

The main body of the chapel, which occupies the first floor, is entered through an antechapel. A wooden screen divides it from the nave, which is topped by Lutyens's sconces which are classical in form and are lit unashamedly by a naked tubular bulb.

The stark and intimate private chapel of Campion Hall, Oxford gives worshippers a place of quiet reflection while remaining connected, by means of internal windows, to the chapel below. Despite its small scale, the architecture has a monumentality akin to the contemporary Liverpool Cathedral.

Small in scale, the altars in both the antechapel and the intimate private chapel, from which internal windows provide a view into the body of the chapel, are monumental in their starkness and geometry. Yet another chapel is reached through an arch at the east end of the main chapel: the Lady Chapel. Suddenly the visitor is transported into a world of spring flowers and tender homely observation, for the walls have been almost entirely covered in murals. They were commissioned in 1941, using royalties from Evelyn Waugh's *Edmund Campion: Jesuit and Martyr*, written as a thank offering to D'Arcy who had been responsible for his conversion; they amounted to £600.

On June 12, 1939, Lutyens visited Middleton Park, in Oxfordshire, which he had designed for Lord Jersey and his film-star wife, Virginia Cherrill, the former Mrs Cary Grant – 'a common little woman without brain' – and went on to the more congenial Campion Hall. There a large party included 'a curiously nice David Jones, a poem writing artist': Lutyens thought he worked on too small a scale, though, to do murals, and suggested Stanley Spencer, who completed his paintings for the Sandham Memorial Chapel at Burghclere in 1932. Spencer, declaring that his painting owed 'nothing to God and everything to the Devil', and prone to obscenity, proved too much for the fathers; in any case, it was clear he would not be prepared to live at Campion Hall for the duration of the project. The Catalonian painter Josep Maria Sert told Lutyens

The Lady Chapel, in contrast to the plain decoration of the nave, was richly decorated in murals by Charles Mohoney. Commissioned in 1941, the artist had been recommended by the then director of the Tate Gallery, Sir John Rothenstein. A small section remained unfinished following a period of ill health.

that he would paint the apse if Lutyens gave him the job of artist at Liverpool Cathedral; Lutyens could not promise to, so the deal was off. Happening to meet Sir John Rothenstein, director of the Tate Gallery, D'Arcy asked his advice. He recommended Charles Mahoney, describing his work as remarkable for its minute observation of Nature, and D'Arcy said 'Done.' His gentle style was particularly suited to the Lady Chapel, whose theme is the life of the Virgin Mary.[3]

Envoi

I N AN ARTICLE FOR *COUNTRY LIFE* WRITTEN IN THE 1930s, Lutyens declared his architectural creed: he was a humanist. In using this term he was probably thinking of Geoffrey Scott's *The Architecture of Humanism*, which first appeared in 1914, went through a second edition ten years later, and was twice reprinted during Lutyens's lifetime. I suspect that Scott's big idea corresponds with Lutyens's philosophy, and it is worth quoting at moderate length. Writing of the masters of the Renaissance, Scott declared:

> Theirs is an architecture which by Mass, Space and Line responds of human physical delight, and by Coherence answers to our thought. These means sufficed them. Given these, they could dispense at will with sculpture and with colour, with academic precedents and poetic fancies, with the strict logic of construction or of use. All those, also, they could employ: but by none of them were they bound. Architecture, based on Humanism, became an independent art.
>
> ... Man, as the savage first conceived him, as the mind of science still affirms, is not the centre of the world he lives in, but merely one of her myriad products, more conscious than the rest and more perplexed. A stranger on the indifferent earth, he adapts himself slowly and painfully to inhuman nature, and at moments, not without peril, compels inhuman nature to his

need. A spectacle surrounds him – sometimes splendid, often morose, uncouth and formidable. He may cower before it like the savage, study it impartially for what it is, like the man of science; it remains, in the end, as in the beginning, something alien and inhuman, often destructive of his hopes. But a third way is open. He may construct, within the world as it is, a pattern of the world as he would have it. This is the way of humanism, in philosophy, in life, and in the arts.

This was surely also the way of Lutyens, a man who was driven to create ideal spaces: lyrical in his early career, elemental and abstract after the First World War.

Lord Halifax, Viceroy of India, saw Lutyens as 'part schoolboy, part great artist, part mystic'. In recent years, the reputation of Ned as the irrepressible joker has tended to overshadow the other two elements of the description, and even admirers who recognise him to have been an architect of extraordinary powers stop short of acknowledging the spiritual profundity of his work. This may be because Lutyens rarely articulated it himself. Except as an inveterate punster, he knew that he was no good at speaking or writing. He was in this respect like a composer who does not talk publicly about the content of his work: if he could say the same thing in words, why would he put himself through the ordeal of writing music? Architecture was Lutyens's language. Only once, as far as we know, did he try to explain the high meaning that it held for him in writing, and that was in a letter to Emily in 1907:

> There is that in art which transcends all rules, it is the divine – I use poor words – and this is what makes all the arts so absorbing and thrilling to follow, creating a furore … there is the same effect produced on all and in all work by a master mind. To short sight it is a miracle, to those a little longer sighted it is

Godhead, if we could see yet better, these facts may be revealed before which the V[ery] God as we conceive him will fade dim.

Truly to understand what Lutyens meant, we must go to the buildings themselves and find what they have to tell us. I hope that this short biography has given some pointers.

Humorous drawing of staff and pupils at work in Lutyens's drawing office, originally the dining room of his house in Bloomsbury Square, 1900. Having ascended the scaffold, Lutyens could (in this fantasy) have reached the family quarters upstairs via the trap door, marked 'E.L.L. only'. Some former pupils became notable architects – Oswald Milne, Paul Phipps – as did Lutyens's own son, Robert.

At Tyringham, Lutyens added two temples either side of a pool to the gardens of the Sir John Soane house. One was a bathing pavilion and the other a Temple of Music. Lutyens would sit in the Temple of Music to contemplate the geometry he had created.

Chronology

1888 Alterations to The Corner, Thursley, Surrey for E. Gray (1890 additions for C.D. Heatley).

1889 Crooksbury, Farnham, Surrey for Arthur Chapman.

· *Leaves George's office to set up his own practice.*

· *Meets Gertrude Jekyll who will later introduce him to HRH Princess Louise, Edward Hudson of Country Life and many other clients. In due course they design over a hundred gardens together.*

1893–5 Chinthurst Hill, Wonersh, Surrey for Miss Aemilia Guthrie.

1894 The Hut, Munstead: a cottage for Gertrude Jekyll which she occupies while Munstead Wood is being built.

1895–6 Munstead Wood for Gertrude Jekyll.

1897 Fulbrook, Surrey for G. Streatfield.

· Berrydown, Hampshire for A. Grove.

· Orchards, Surrey for Sir William Chance.

· The Pleasaunce, Norfolk for Lord Battersea.

· *Marries Lady Emily Lytton*

1898 British Pavilion for the Paris Exhibition of 1900.

1899 Le Bois des Moutiers at Varengeville, Normandy for Guillaume Mallet.

· Goddards, Abinger, Surrey for Sir Frederick Mirrielees (wings added 1909–10).

· Deanery Garden, Berkshire for Edward Hudson.

· Tigbourne Court, Witley, Surrey for Edgar Horne.

1900 Homewood, Knebworth, Hertfordshire, for his mother-in-law, the Dowager Countess of Lytton.

1901–4 Marsh Court, Hampshire, for Herbert Johnson (stables 1905; Great Room added 1924–6).

1901 Greywalls, Gullane, for the Hon. Alfred Lyttelton.

1902 Little Thakeham, Sussex for Ernest M. Blackburn.

· Monkton House, Singleton, Sussex for William James.

· Lindisfarne Castle, Northumberland for Edward Hudson.

1903 Daneshill, Basing, Hampshire, for Walter Hoare.

1904 Country Life Offices, Tavistock Street, London for Edward Hudson.

· Ashby St Ledgers, Northamptonshire, for the Hon. Ivor Guest (alterations, gardens and buildings on the estate 1904–38).

1905 Nashdom, Buckinghamshire for Prince and Princess Alexis Dolgorouki.

· Lambay Castle, Ireland for Hon. C. Baring (Lord Revelstoke).

1906 Heathcote, Ilkley, Yorkshire for John Thomas Hemingway.

· Folly Farm, Berkshire, for H. Cochrane.

· New Place, Hampshire, for Mrs A.S. Franklyn.

- Offices for The Garden, No. 42 Kingsway, London, for William Robinson.
- The Dormy House, Walton Heath Golf Club, Surrey for G.A. Riddell.

1908 *Appointed architect for Hampstead Garden Suburb, where he designed the Central Square including* the Institute, St Jude on the Hill and the Free Church.
- Temple Dinsley, Hertfordshire (enlargement) for H.G. Fenwick.
- Middlefield, Cambridge for Henry Bond.
- Whalton Manor, Northumberland (remodelling) for Eustace Smith.

1910–30 Castle Drogo, Drewsteignton, Devon for Julius Drewe.

1911 The Salutation, Sandwich, Kent and No. 7, St James's Square, London for Henry Farrer.
- No. 36 Smith Square, London for the Rt. Hon. Reginald McKenna.
- Theosophical Society's Headquarters, Tavistock Square, London for Mrs Annie Besant (extended 1923 for the British Medical Association Headquarters).
- The Corner House, Cowley Street, London for Major the Rt. Hon. Sir Henry and Lady Norman.
- No. 8 Little College Street, Westminster, London for The Hon. F. W. Maclaren.

1911–12 Rand Regiments Memorial, Johannesburg.

1912–16 Additions for Folly Farm, Sulhamstead, Berkshire for Zachary Merton.
- Ednaston Manor, Derbyshire, for William G. Player.
- Johannesburg Art Gallery for the Corporation of Johannesburg.
- British School at Rome for Sir Rennell Rodd (originally a pavilion for the Rome International Exhibition of 1911).

1912 *Elected a member of the Delhi Planning Commission; sets sail for India on the first of nineteen journeys to plan the new city. Begins designs for the Viceroy's House, New Delhi (also Viceroy's Court, fountains etc).*

1913 Abbey House, Barrow-in-Furness, Lancashire for Messrs Vickers.

1917–18 *Appointed one of three Principal Architects to the Imperial War Graves Commission, with Herbert Baker and Reginald Blomfield.* Works include:
- The War Stone (1917)
- Étaples Military Cemetery (1919)
- Memorial to the Missing and Cemetery, Faubourg d'Amiens, Arras (1924–5)
- Memorial to the Missing of the Somme, Thiepval (1926–7)
- Villers-Bretonneux Military Cemetery, Somme (c.1927–38)

1918 *Knighted for his work at New Delhi and the Imperial War Graves Commission.*

1919 Temporary Cenotaph, Whitehall, London for the Rt. Hon. David Lloyd George.

1920 Permanent Cenotaph at Whitehall.
- Britannic House, London for the Anglo-Persian Oil Company.
- *Elected Royal Academician.*

1921 HM Queen Mary's Dolls' House (exhibited 1924).
- *Awarded the Royal Gold Medal by the Royal Institute of British Architects.*

1922 Midland Bank Piccadilly Branch, London for Rt. Hon. Reginald McKenna.

1924 All India War Memorial Arch, New Delhi.

1924–39 Midland Bank Head Office, Poultry, London for Rt. Hon. Reginald McKenna.

1925 Park House, Mells, Somerset for Rt. Hon. Reginald McKenna.

1925–7 Gledstone Hall, Yorkshire for Sir Amos Nelson.

1926 Garden and two pavilions, Tyringham House, Buckinghamshire for Frederick Konig.

· Palace for the Nizam of Hyderabad, New Delhi.

1927 British Embassy in Washington, D.C., U.S.A.

· Plumpton Place, East Sussex (alterations) for Edward Hudson.

1928 Midland Bank Leadenhall Street Branch, London for Rt. Hon. Reginald McKenna.

· Flats in Page Street and Vincent Street, London, for Westminster City Council.

1928–9 No. 67–68 Pall Mall, London for Victor Behar.

1929 Midland Bank King Street Branch, Manchester for Rt. Hon Reginald McKenna.

· Commission for the Liverpool Metropolitan Cathedral by the Most Rev. Richard Downey, Archbishop of Liverpool.

1929–31 No. 120 Pall Mall, London for Crane Bennett Ltd.

1930 YWCA Central Club, Great Russell Street, London.

· Landscape, bridges and lodges at Runnymede, Surrey for Cara Broughton, Lady Fairhaven.

· *Created Knight Commander of the Order of the Indian Empire (KCIE).*

1933–41 Crypt at the Liverpool Metropolitan Cathedral.

1935 Reuters, 85 Fleet Street, London for Sir Roderick Jones.

· Campion Hall, Oxford for the Society of Jesus.

1937–9 Admiral Beatty and Admiral Jellicoe memorial fountains, Trafalgar Square, London.

1938 Middleton Park, Oxfordshire for the Earl of Jersey.

· Halnaker House, Halnaker, West Sussex, for the Rt. Hon. Reginald McKenna.

· Australian Memorial at Villers-Bretonneux.

· *Elected President of the Royal Academy.*

1939–42 Works on the Royal Academy Plan for London for the Royal Academy of Arts.

1941–3 Works on re-planning of Kingston upon Hull with Sir Patrick Abercrombie.

1942 *Awarded the Order of Merit (OM), the first time an architect had received this honour.*

1944 *Dies on New Year's Day.*

Endnotes

.

INTRODUCTION

1   The mathematics of Lutyens's roof construction is discussed in Hugh Petter's 'The Great Game: The Classical Architecture of Sir Edwin Lutyens', *L'architettura delle città. The Journal of the Scientific Society Ludovico Quaroni*, vol. 4, no. 7 (2015), pp. 31–44.

2   E.L. Lutyens, 'The Work of the Late Philip Webb,' *Country Life*, May 8, 1915, p. 618.

3   It is now moot whether the chairs were actually designed by Lutyens: I am grateful to Candia Lutyens for observing that they are a direct copy of a Sheraton example illustrated in vol. 3 of Percy Macquoid's *History of English Furniture* which appeared in 1906.

4   His views are expressed in one of his few articles, 'What I Think of Modern Architecture', *Country Life*, June 20, 1931, pp. 775–7.

5   In Spain, Lutyens designed several largely unexecuted projects during and after the First World War for members of the ultra-rich, Francoist family of the Duke of Alba.

6   Jane Ridley, *The Architect and his Wife: A Life of Edwin Lutyens*, 2002, p. 332.

7   See Timothy Brittain-Catlin, *The Edwardians and their Houses: The New Life of Old England*, 2020, *passim*.

8   Judy Neiswander, *The Cosmopolitan Interior: Liberalism and the British Home*, 2008, p. 53.

9   See G. A. Bremner (ed.), *Architecture and Urbanism in the British Empire*, 2016, p. 150.

10   Mary Lutyens, *Edwin Lutyens by his Daughter*, 1980, p. 245.

11   Daphne Pollen, *I Remember, I Remember*, privately published, 2008, p. 164. With thanks to Louis Jebb.

I. THE SURREY HILLS

1   The reminiscence appears in the typescript *Some Recorded Details of the Lutyens Family 1700–1950*, collected by E.J.T. Lutyens in 1954 (unpublished). Now in the possession of Mark Lutyens.

2   Violet Stuart-Wortley, *Grow Old Along With Me: Reminiscences*, 1952, p. 24.

3   George Sturt, *Change in the Village*, 1912, p. 116.

4   Brown, *Lutyens and the Edwardians*, 1996, p. 5.

5   I am grateful to Dr Robin Prater for sharing her knowledge of Lutyens's neo-Georgian work.

6   I am grateful to Hugh Petter who has a collection of such manuals.
7   Stuart-Wortley, *Grow Old Along With Me*, p. 31.
8   For more information, see John Stewart, *Sir Herbert Baker: Architect to the British Empire*, 2021.
9   We know this from the rare obituary that Lutyens wrote of Webb in *Country Life* (May 8, 1915, p. 618.)
10 John Aplin (ed.), *The Letters of Philip Webb*, vol. 4, 2015, p. 134; 'Great Tangley Manor, Surrey', *Country Life*, January 21, 1905, p. 94.
11 Clayre Percy and Jane Ridley (eds), *The Letters of Edwin Lutyens to his Wife, Lady Emily*, 1985, pp. 11–12.
12 Quoted in Michael Tooley, 'Gertrude Jekyll (1843–1932)', *Oxford Dictionary of National Biography*, <www.oxforddnb.com>.
13 For J.J. Stevenson and his family, see Hew Stevenson, *Jobs for the Boys: The Story of a Family in Britain's Imperial Heyday*, 2009.
14 Quoted in John Brandon Jones, 'Reminiscences on Sir Edwin Lutyens', *Architectural Association Journal*, vol. 74, no. 823 (June 1956), p. 226. Lutyens makes the comment in the context of a tribute to Voysey: 'Simple old-world forms, moulded to his own passion, as if an old testament had been rewrit in vivid print, bringing to light a renewed vision in turning its pages, an old world made new.'
15 See Gertrude Jekyll, *Home and Garden: Notes and Thoughts, Practical and Critical, of a Worker in Both*, 1900, pp. 16–17

2. OH EMY IT'S SPLENDID

1   I am grateful to Peter O'Donoghue, York Herald, for explaining Lutyens's coat of arms, granted to him on August 4, 1936. It is 'described heraldically as Sable the stone Capital of a Pillar Argent on a Chief Or between two Saltires a Rose Gules barbed and seeded proper and for the crest On a Wreath Two concentric Annulets Azure charged with three Mullets Agent. That is a black shield with a silver-coloured stone capital of a pillar, the top part of the shield in gold with a red rose with naturally-coloured seeds and sepals, flanked on either side by a red saltire. The crest (the part above the helmet which has the visor open and faces the front to denote a knight) stands on a wreath of twisted silk in alternating black and silver and is formed of two concentric blue rings, with three five-pointed silver stars laid on top.' The motto is Lutyens's favourite METIENDO VIVENDUM – By Measure We Must Live.
2   Ridley, *The Architect and his Wife*, p. 94.
3   For example, on February 10, 1899, he complained to Lady Emily about the 'bad service' provided by Frederick Mirrielees, his client at Goddards: 'I mean you go to dress and find your bag not unpacked and in the morning the maid knocks timidly at one's door leaving cans and boots outside in timid propriety. Such a bore!'

3. BOOM IT LIKE ANYTHING

1   F. Scott Fitzgerald, *The Crack-Up*, ed. Edmund Wilson, 2009, p. 69.
2   From 'Edward Hudson', a chapter of an unpublished memoir by Noel Carrington given to the present author in around 1980.

3   Bernard Darwin, *Fifty Years of 'Country Life'*, 1947, p. 40.
4   Edward Hudson to Gertrude Jekyll September 25, 1929. Edward Hudson's correspondence with Gertrude Jekyll about Plumpton Place is in the Gertrude Jekyll Collection at the University of California at Berkeley. Thanks to a grant from the Surrey and Sussex Garden Trust, it has been digitised and can be found at <https://calisphere.org/>, 'Plumpton Place', items 25–56.
5   See Gavin Stamp, 'An Architectural Revelation: Berrydown Court, Overton, Hampshire', *Country Life*, June 12, 2013, pp. 64ff.; 'A House Beyond the Pale: Chinthurst Hill, Surrey [I]', ibid., March 18, 2015, pp. 84–8; 'Childhood Imaginings: Chinthurst Hill [II]', ibid., March 25, 2015, pp. 52–7.

4. TIGER, TIGER

1   Until recently, Johnnie seemed, to quote Jane Brown, to have 'melted into the anonymity of the years'. He has now been rescued from this obscurity by Francis James's *Marsh Court: The Missing Chapters*, 2015.

5. WHAT FUN IT WOULD BE

1   Pollen, *I Remember, I Remember*, p. 48.
2   Pollen, *I Remember, I Remember*, p. 162.
3   Percy and Ridley, *Letters of Edwin Lutyens to his Wife*, p. 169.
4   Brown, *Lutyens and the Edwardians: An English Architect and his Clients*, 1996, p. 131.
5   John Goodall, 'Prospero's Isle', *Country Life*, October 19 and 26, 2016, pp. 50–57.
6   Percy and Ridley, *Letters of Edwin Lutyens to his Wife*, p. 197.
7   Ibid., p. 287.

6. THE HIGH GAME

1   'Duty Done to Charities During Lifetime. Bradford Merchant and his Fortune', *The Manchester Guardian*, December 16, 1926, p. 12.
2   J.M. Bryden, 'The English Renaissance', *The Builder*, vol. 56, no. 2404 (March 2, 1889), p. 169, quoted in G.A. Bremner, *Building Greater Britain: Architecture, Imperialism, and the Edwardian Baroque Revival, 1885–1920*, 2022, p. 18.
3   Lawrence Weaver, 'Ardenrun Place, Blindlet Heath, Surrey, The Residence of Mr H. H. Konig', *Country Life*, January 21, 1911, p. 95.
4   *The Builder*, November 19, 1904, p. 523.

7. INDESTRUCTIBLE, SEVERE AND MAGNIFICENT

1   'Memoirs of Beatrice Foster Drewe, née Newington, and Mrs Frances Young, youngest daughter of Julius Drewe', East Sussex Record Office, Brighton, ACC 10210/37.
2   I am grateful to Rebecca Lilley for information on the Turkish bath.
3   On Walker's death in 1934, Lutyens wrote to condole with his widow for the death

of a husband 'who did so much invaluable work for me, and with whom I had looked forward to the opportunity of doing more'.

4 For more on Castle Drogo, see Peter Inskip, 'The Compromise of Castle Drogo', *Architectural Review*, vol. 165 (1979), pp. 220–26.

8. BYZANTINE-CUM-NEDI

1 Andrew Saint, 'Unwin, Sir Raymond (1863–1940)', *Oxford Dictionary of National Biography*.
2 Henrietta Barnett, *The Story of the Growth of the Hampstead Garden Suburb, 1907–1928*, 1928, p. 6.
3 Henrietta Barnett, *Story of the Growth of the Hampstead Garden Suburb*; quoted in Mervyn Miller, *Hampstead Garden Suburb: Arts and Crafts Utopia?*, 2006, p. 123.
4 Henrietta Barnett, *Canon Barnett …: His Life, Work, and Friends*, 1919, vol. 2, p. 376.
5 Mervyn Miller and A. Stuart Grey, *Hampstead Garden Suburb*, 1992, p. 85.

9. WREN COULD NEVER HAVE DONE THIS

1 Henry Sharp, *Good-bye India*, 1946, p. 181.
2 Carl Peters, *England and the English*, 1904, pp. 60, 62.
3 Obituary, 'Dr H.V. Lanchester,' *The Times*, January 17, 1953, p. 8.
4 Jane Ridley, 'Edwin Lutyens, New Delhi and the Architecture of Imperialism', *The Journal of Imperial and Commonwealth History*, vol. 26, no. 2 (May 1998), p. 72.
5 Quoted in Christopher Hussey, *The Life of Sir Edwin Lutyens*, 1950, pp. 277 and Gavin Stamp, 'New Delhi', in Colin Amery et al. (eds), *Lutyens: The Work of the English Architect Sir Edwin Lutyens 1869–1944*, 1981, p. 37.
6 S[igismund] D[avid] Waley, *Edwin Montagu: A Memoir and an Account of His Visits to India*, 1964, p. 325.
7 Gavin Stamp, 'British Architecture in India, 1857–1947', *Journal of the Royal Society of Arts*, vol. 129 (1981), p. 358.
8 Stewart, *Herbert Baker*, p. 114.
9 See Íñigo Basarrate, 'Edwin Lutyens in Spain: The Palace of El Guadalperal', *Architectural History*, vol. 60 (2017), pp. 303–39.
10 Philip Davies, *Splendours of the Raj: British Architecture in India 1660–1947*, 1985, p. 229.
11 I am grateful to Mary Miers for introducing me to Rosehaugh.
12 Stewart, *Herbert Baker*, p. 127.

10. KNOWN UNTO GOD

1 Hugh Petter, *Lutyens in Italy*, 1992, p. 40.
2 Allan Greenberg, 'Lutyens's Cenotaph', *Journal of the Society of Architectural Historians*, vol. 48, no. 1 (March 1989), pp. 5–23.
3 The Hispano-English Committee, 'Summary of the Lecture which Sir Edwin Lutyens will give in the auditorium of La Residencia de Estudiantes, Madrid, on Thursday 14th June 1934 at 7.00 pm'. Courtesy of the Lutyens Trust; <https://www.lutyenstrust.org.uk/portfolio-item/the-hispano-english-committee/>.

4 Quoted in Greenberg, 'Lutyens's Cenotaph', p. 11.
5 Quoted by Fabian Ware in 'Building and Decoration of the War Cemeteries,' *Journal of the Royal Society of Arts*, vol.72 (April 11, 1924), pp. 344–55.

11. I DON'T KNOW WHAT YOU MEAN BY 'ABOUT'

1 Martin Farr, *Reginald McKenna: Financier among Statesmen, 1863–1916*, 2008, p. 24.
2 Ibid., p. 17.
3 'In the Winning Crew' (Spy), *Vanity Fair*, October 31, 1906.
4 April 12, 1937.
5 Quoted in Brown, *Lutyens and the Edwardians*, pp. 108–9.
6 The Pamela McKenna letters, undated, are in the Churchill Archives Centre at Cambridge.
7 Margot Asquith, *The Autobiography of Margot Asquith*, 1920, p. 191.
8 Frances Horner, *Time Remembered*, 1933, p. 202.
9 Queen Mary's Dolls' House was exhibited at the 1924 British Empire Exhibition at Wembley and can now be seen in Windsor Castle.
10 Jane Brown, *Lutyens and The Edwardians*, p. 220.
11 *Landmarks in Piccadilly 1685–1925*. Courtesy of HSBC Archive.
12 Quoted in *The Midland Venture: The Magazine of the Midland Bank Staff Association*, vol. 5, issue 58 (December 1924), p. 416.
13 Edwin Green, *Buildings for Bankers: Sir Edward Lutyens and the Midland Bank, 1921–1939*, 1980, p. 7. See also Green, *The House of Midland: A Guide to Midland Bank Head Office*, 1990.
14 Green, *Buildings for Bankers*, p. 16.
15 Ibid., p. 20.
16 Hussey, *Life of Sir Edwin Lutyens*, p. 471.
17 *The Midland Venture*, vol. 16, issue 187 (September 1925), p. 343.
18 A.R. Holmes and Edwin Green, *Midland: 150 Years of Banking Business*, 1986, pp. 175–6.

12. THE BIGGEST DOME IN CHRISTENDOM

1 Ridley, *The Architect and his Wife*, p. 370; see also 'Liverpool's New Cathedral. Sir Edwin Lutyens Interviewed', *The Observer*, May 28, 1933, p. 11.
2 Robert Lutyens, Correspondence: 'The New Liverpool Cathedral', *Country Life*, March 3, 1955, p. 629.
3 'Liverpool's New Cathedral: Papal Legate on "a Resounding Answer". 25,000 at Consecration Ceremony', *The Manchester Guardian*, June 6, 1933, p. 16.
4 Ridley, *The Architect and his Wife*, p. 384; 'Reminiscences on Sir Edwin Lutyens', *Architectural Association Journal*, vol. 74 (1959), pp. 226–36.
5 For further reading for Liverpool Metropolitan Cathedral, see G. Hasling, 'Liverpool Metropolitan Cathedral: Comparison of the Scott & Lutyens Designs', *The Builder*, vol. 188 (March 4, 1955), pp. 366–9; Christopher Hussey, 'The Cathedral of Christ the King, Liverpool: Sir Edwin Lutyens's Model at the Royal Academy', *Country Life*, 8 May 1934, pp. 451–4; John Summerson, 'Arches of Triumph: The Design for Liverpool Cathedral', in *The Unromantic Castle*, 1990, pp 245–56.

13. WHY NOT ASK ME?

1 H.J.A. Sire, *Father Martin D'Arcy: Philosopher of Christian Love* (1997), p. 80.
2 William S. Abell (ed.), *Laughter and the Love of Friends: Reminiscences of the Distinguished English Priest and Philosopher Martin Cyril D'Arcy, S.J.*, 1991. Quoted in David Frazer Lewis, *Lutyens's Designs for Campion Hall, Oxford*, Twentieth Century Architecture, vol. 11 (2013), pp. 52–65.
3 For further reading on Campion Hall, see Lewis, 'Lutyens's Designs for Campion Hall, Oxford', ibid., and Geoffrey Tyack, 'Baker and Lutyens in Oxford: The Building of Rhodes House and Campion Hall', *Oxoniensia*, vol. 62 (1997), pp 287–308.

Further Reading

Amery, Colin, and Margaret Richardson (eds). *Lutyens*, Hayward Gallery exh. cat. 1981.

Aslet, Clive. *The Last Country Houses*. 1982

Aslet, Clive. *The Edwardian Country House*. 2012

Aslet, Clive. *War Memorial: The Story of One Village's Sacrifice from 1914 to 2003*. 2013

Brittain-Catlin, Timothy. *The Edwardians and their Houses: The New Life of Old England*. 2020

Brown, Jane. *Gardens of a Golden Afternoon, The Story of a Partnership: Edwin Lutyens and Gertrude Jekyll*. 1982

Brown, Jane. *Lutyens and the Edwardians: An English Architect and his Clients*. 1996

Budgen, Christopher. *West Surrey Architecture 1840–2000*. 2002

Butler, A.S.G. *The Architecture of Sir Edwin Lutyens*, 3 vols. 1950 (*The Lutyens Memorial Volumes*: Country Life Books, vols 1–3)

Cole, David. *Sir Edwin Lutyens: The Arts and Crafts Houses*. 2017

Geurst, Jeroen. *Cemeteries of the Great War by Edwin Lutyens*. 2010

Ghosh, Nijit, and School of Planning and Architecture, New Delhi. *The Making of New Delhi*, exh. cat. 1980

Gradidge, Roderick. *Edwin Lutyens: Architect Laureate*. 1981

Gradidge, Roderick. *The Surrey Style*. 1991

Hussey, Christopher. *The Life of Sir Edwin Lutyens*. 1950 (*The Lutyens Memorial Volumes*: Country Life Books, vol. 4)

Inskip, Peter. *Edwin Lutyens* (Architectural Monographs, No. 6). 1979

Irving, Robert Grant. *Indian Summer: Lutyens, Baker and Imperial Delhi*. 1981

Jekyll, Gertrude. *Home and Garden*. 1900

Jekyll, Gertrude. *Old West Surrey*. 1940

Lambton, Lucinda. *The Queen's Dolls' House*. 2010

Lutyens, Mark. *'Lut': Life in the Office of Sir Edwin Lutyens*. 2022

Lutyens, Mary. *Edwin Lutyens by his Daughter*. 1980

Lutyens, Mary. *Krishnamurti: The Years of Awakening*. 1984

Lutyens, Robert. *Six Great Architects: Inigo Jones, Wren, Vanbrugh, the Adam Brothers, Nash, Sir Edwin Lutyens*. 1959

Miller, Mervyn. *Hampstead Garden Suburb Past and Present*. 1995

O'Neill, Daniel. *Sir Edwin Lutyens: Country Houses*. 1980

Percy, Clayre, and Jane Ridley (eds). *The Letters of Edwin Lutyens*. 1985

Rambert, Frank. *Gardens of War: British Cemeteries on the Western Front*. 2014 (also published in French as *Jardins de guerre*)

Richardson, Margaret. *Sketches by Edwin Lutyens*. 1994

Ridley, Jane. *The Architect and His Wife*. 2002

Singh, Malvika. *New Delhi: Making of a Capital*. 2009

Skelton, Tim, and Gerald Gliddon. *Lutyens and the Great War*. 2008

Stamp, Gavin. *Lutyens: Country Houses. From the Archives of Country Life.* 2001
Stamp, Gavin. *The Memorial to the Missing of the Somme.* 2006
Tankard, Judith, and Martin A. Wood. *Gertrude Jekyll at Munstead Wood.* 1996
Volwahsen, Andreas. *Imperial Delhi.* 2002
Weaver, Lawrence. *Houses and Gardens by Edwin Lutyens.* 1913

Readers wanting to pursue their interest in Lutyens are recommended to join The Lutyens Trust (*www.lutyenstrust.org.uk*) or The Lutyens Trust America (*www.lutyenstrustamerica. com*).

Picture Credits

Front cover: © *Country Life*, Future Publishing Ltd
Endpapers: © Carl Laubin
25: © Ben Hatherell, Lutyens Trust Photo Archive
29: © The Lutyens Family
39: © Dylan Thomas
42 top: © *Country Life*, Future Publishing Ltd
42 bottom: © Dylan Thomas
45–46: © Dylan Thomas
50: © The Lutyens Family
54–55: © Dylan Thomas/Private Collection
57: © Knebworth House Estate
60: © *Country Life*, Future Publishing Ltd
62: © Dylan Thomas
63: © The Lutyens Family
69: © RIBA Collections
71–72: © *Country Life*, Future Publishing Ltd
73: © National Trust Images/Andreas von Einsiedel
74: © National Trust Images/511937
78: © Andrew Barnett, Lutyens Trust Photo Archive
79: © The Lutyens Family
84: © Country Life Books
89 top & bottom: © Knight Frank, Lutyens Trust Photo Archive
91: © *Country Life*, Future Publishing Ltd
93: © Country Life Books
94–101: © Will Pryce, *Country Life*, Future Publishing Ltd
102: © René de Wit
105: © RIBA Collections
109 top: © Country Life Books
109 bottom: © Andrew Barnett, Lutyens Trust Photo Archive
114: © Cloud 9 Leeds / RIBA Collections
116: © Andrew Barnett, Lutyens Trust Photographic Archive
118: © Courtesy of the Drewe Family
120–121: © Dylan Thomas, *Country Life*, Future Publishing Ltd
126: © Country Life Books
136: © RIBA Collections
139: © Dylan Thomas
142–143: © RIBA Collections
146: © The Lutyens Family
153: © Private Collection/Bridgeman Images

Index